JUSTIN WEBB

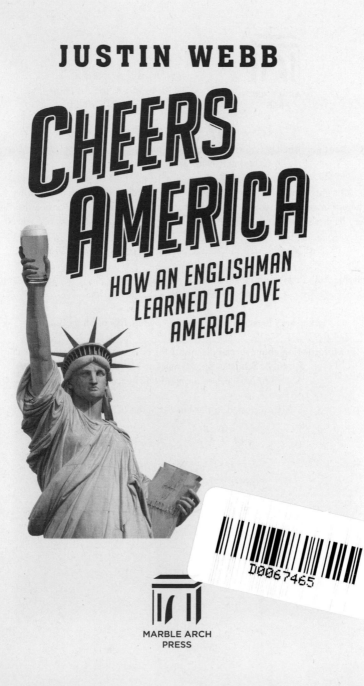

CHEERS AMERICA

HOW AN ENGLISHMAN LEARNED TO LOVE AMERICA

MARBLE ARCH
PRESS

**MARBLE ARCH
PRESS**

Marble Arch Press
1230 Avenue of the Americas
New York, NY 10020

First Marble Arch Press trade paperback edition March 2013

Marble Arch Press is a publishing collaboration between Short Books, UK, and Atria Books, US.

Marble Arch Press and colophon are trademarks of Short Books.

For information about special discounts for bulk purchases, please contact Simon & Schuster Special Sales at 1-866-506-1949 or business@simonandschuster.com

Manufactured in the United States of America

10 9 8 7 6 5 4 3 2 1

ISBN 978-1-4767-3019-6
ISBN 978-1-4767-3020-2 (ebook)

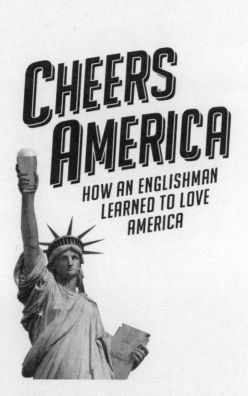

CHEERS AMERICA

HOW AN ENGLISHMAN LEARNED TO LOVE AMERICA

To Sarah, Sam, Martha and Clara

Contents

Chapter One

SAY *WHAAAT????*

The response – I paraphrase it here – of most English men and women to Mitt Romney's overtures in the summer of 2012 puzzled and wrongfooted the then GOP presidential candidate, but served a decent purpose nonetheless. It told a big truth about You (the Americans) and Us (the English). An adviser had suggested that Mr Romney was keen to rebuild America's ties with those he called "Anglo-Saxons". He had thought the use of this phrase would be helpful, a harmless tickling of the tummies of the stuffy old English as they pottered about their quaint Tudor homes making tea and trying, still, to find a role after losing that Empire.

But that term– Anglo-Saxons – blew up in Mr Romney's face. In America, contrasting the candidate of the Anglo-Saxons against a president who did not look hugely like a *Mayflower* settler caused a certain queasiness. But in England, the supposed home of the genus Anglo-Saxon, there was even greater incredulity. How could a serious candidate for high office in the United States possibly look at England, and in particular our capital city, and think of it as Anglo-Saxon? How could he think of us as Anglo-Saxon? How could that formulation seriously have meaning for anyone but a few crackpots in the modern age? What was he (or his adviser) thinking?

The truth is that England is more Anglo-Saxon than, say, San Antonio, Texas. The idea that some Americans, and more importantly some American ideas, come from England, is not wrong, of course, and perfectly worthy of celebration; though I shall argue in the serious bits of this book that the transmutation of many of those ideas across the Atlantic has included more of the mutation than the trans, if you get my drift. Still, we do have a common heritage, and although America has just been through an election cycle with no white Protestant in either of the presidential tickets, or leading the Senate or the House, or indeed represented on the Supreme Court, there is still plainly a link of sorts between what you came from (us) and what you have become (you)... but my point in this book is to tell the story of how that link is fading and why allowing it to fade gently and with dignity would be a good thing for both sides. For England and the English the prize would be – ironically – independence after years of fawning over the special relationship; for America the prize would be the grasping of the nettle that Mitt Romney did not want to grasp: not that Americans at home should be more Anglo-Saxon (he knows as well as anyone this ain't gonna happen), but that a world-view that sees those who are steeped in this tradition (plus Israel) as being the bedrock of America's network of alliances must change; this is a world in which new nations, or old nations reborn as in the case of China, are the driving force of global growth and increasingly of global power and diplomacy. America needs to manage its decline – not an absolute decline as the gloom-mongers and the anti-Americans predict and hope (we will return to this later) but a relative decline based on the fact, and it is a fact, that other nations are growing at rates that the West cannot match and will not match in the foreseeable future. These nations need not be appeased when they are evil or aped when they are mistaken but they do need to be approached seriously. America's relationship with China is far more important than its relationship with England. We English need to grasp this as much as you Americans do.

A break with England will also persuade you to face up to one of the great questions of our times, which the rise of China poses in the starkest terms: when nations develop do they, as night follows day, become more democratic and more Western, in the sense of taking on modern Western attitudes towards tolerance and pluralism and the rule of law? Or is there another way – a Chinese way, you could call it – in which economic development will lead China and the nations in her sphere of influence into a position of world economic leadership (China will probably overtake America as the world's biggest economy within the next few decades) without the underpinnings of democracy? The Chinese government is certainly competent and efficient, and you could argue that it is legitimate as well – there is no Arab Spring groundswell of discontent in China – but is Chinese authoritarianism a feasible long-term plan? Should America fear being overtaken by a nation that simply rejects American values and refuses to become more American as it gets richer? What should America do in those circumstances?

Might Americans in 2050 be arguing for five-year plans set by Washington and less transparency and freedom for businesses in the national interest? Or will (as most Americans suspect) the Chinese model simply prove a useful transitional tool which loses its usefulness once the job of getting rich is done? These questions will need to be addressed with a degree of subtlety and sure-footedness that can only come from real concentration and effort – and self confidence as well. America's relationship with China is the centre-piece of 21st-century diplomacy – the biggest favour the English can do their cousins (and themselves) is to get you folks to turn around and look west, not east; English people should be shouting out loud like kids at a pantomime: "It's BEHIND YOU!" Bugger the special relationship with us – the special relation-ship you need to develop – a much more complex one – is with the nations across the Pacific who will, led by China, dominate the world in the future.

This is not – I should say loud and clear at the very start – an official BBC view of the relationship between the UK and the US. It is a view entirely my own, though it is based very firmly in the work I did for the BBC during my eight years as its chief reporter in America. In that time I travelled widely.

I covered presidential campaigns and midterm elections, I gripped and grinned with George W. Bush and sat down for a full-length interview with President Obama, but more importantly I covered the wider political and social culture of the US; the demise of the rural Greyhound service in Texas, the extraordinary work being done by evangelicals in prisons in Arkansas, the glory and danger of the American outdoors, the mystery (to our eyes) of your patriotism, your love of guns, and the way you use the language you call English. As a reporter I talked to dumb Americans and smart Americans. Also to Americans of every shape and size. I mention shape and size because I also tried during my time in the US to combat some of the sickly prejudices the English sometimes have about the US. Many Americans are not fat. This was a surprise to English audiences. Most American towns are more peaceful than most English towns: this too was a shock. American politics does involve real choice between serious alternatives: again a surprise to the English. But I also came to believe what many of you Americans believe about yourselves and your political culture: it is broken, pretty fundamentally broken. It can be fixed and it might be fixed and it should be fixed, for the good of us all, but it is, at the moment, unfixed. Part of the process of fixing America, I shall argue, is ditching pretences, including the pretence that we are your best friends forever.

My family and I lived in Washington DC, and my daughter Clara was born there. Thus, through her US citizenship, we came home with more than happy memories, of reportage and of life; we also have a US citizen in our midst: we are part of you and you are part of us. Clara wants to live in Hollywood and one day, if she can fix the details, she will sail through the US citizens channel at LAX and take up her birthright. This gives me what you Americans call skin in the game, and we British, rougher folk that we are, call "a dog in the fight". It also gives me a sense of affection for a nation that welcomed her into the world and said to her on day one, at Sibley Hospital in Northwest, Washington DC, have a nice day, and a nice life, and seriously meant it.

She will return – the rest of the family will not. The adventure is over. Many of our American friends found that fact oddly, and interestingly, unsettling.

For America was not designed to be left. The opposite, in fact – it was designed to be arrived in. It was, in the words of the great Eagles song "Hotel California", "programmed to receive" and – as was the case in The Eagles' song – there is some wonderment at the front desk when you try to go.

When our time came to leave, we approached the checkout with typical Englishness. For effect, we exaggerated our sadness at the end of our time in America. The result? Confusion.

"Our British home is in south London so we'll probably all be murdered before Christmas," we said to friends.

"Oh, my gosh. Um, why not stay?" they replied, anxiously.

Because you have no sense of humour, would be one answer. But that (while being partly true) is not fair. Like so many other misunderstimations of you by us and us by you, it hangs there, unchallenged, in the ether. In eight years of life in America, I came to value – to love, actually – the stolid, sunny, unchallenging, simple virtuousness of the American suburban psyche. But back in England, as well as being reintroduced to the darkness, to the can't-do spirit, to what I saw from afar as the drunken directionlessness of our national life, I have seen a side to Britain that I had (to my shame) rather forgotten existed. It's a richness born of knowing, rather than hoping. Contentedness rather than striving. And, as that Olympic ceremony showed in the summer of 2012, yes, humour.

The woman who was to sell our house in Washington was a prime specimen of Americana. She was hellishly perky. Nothing got her down, not even the fact that we were selling in the midst of the biggest depression since the Great Flood. In this area it was different.

"You have a lovely home!"

But she thought we had too many books. She did not say so but she talked of creating spaces on the shelves – for snow-globes, perhaps, or silver photo frames filled with perfect children showing off perfect teeth.

This is a cultural thing. When selling a home in America, you have to pretend that you do not live there. In fact, you have to pretend that no one lives there. Or ever has. Previously owned homes are of course the norm for us Europeans. We understand that other generations have made their mark, lived their lives and passed on to the great home in the sky. This means – as we English know, having grown up with rattling windows and mouldy grouting and those ghosts of the past – that no home will be perfect. You do not make such allowances in America.

So the inspector's report into our Washington house, the survey, was the cause of much deliberation and soul-searching from our potential buyers. An outside light was not working properly. A tap was leaking. A chimney needed investigation. As I read it, my mind turned to our house in London, which is actually falling down – somebody omitted to prop up the middle when an arch was cut in a downstairs room 100 years ago – but which is still eminently saleable. The English understand that *we are all falling down*. Dust to dust, we intuit. Americans do not. You have not got there yet.

In the months before we left the US, I paid the highest tribute to my sense of Americanness: I visited a full-body scanning clinic whose CT X-ray scans were advertised on local radio. These scans are part and parcel of American life in the well-to-do suburbs of the bigger cities. They use high-powered technology that in Britain is the preserve of hospitals and truly ill people. In America you can simply go to your local mall, pay a hefty fee and, in theory, leave armed with a set of scans that tell you precisely how your body is ticking along. The company motto might well epitomise the attitude to life of the whole nation: "Now you have the power to see your future and change it." The phrase is the copyright possession of Virtual Physical of Rockville, Maryland, so if you are a family doctor about to take control of your own budgets in Cleethorpes, England, do not on any account use it. Ah, but of course you wouldn't. Not in a million years. You wouldn't make that claim, and no Brit would believe you if you did.

Truth be told, while I lived in America I decided I would rather be you than us. I admired the concern over the chimney and the belief that any problem (even those associated with my fast-declining body) could be fixed. Before I left, I sat one evening on the porch, in the growing heat of the Washington spring, listening to the cicadas chirruping and the sound of lawns being mowed, and yearned to be staying. It would be so easy, so uncomplicated, so safe. One phrase in particular from the folder I took home from Virtual Physical in Rockville caught my imagination: "Examination of the brain reveals no definite abnormalities!" Had it been otherwise, were it to be otherwise in the future, the implication is that these abnormalities would be zapped faster that you could say "Take me home to my white picket fences". How comforting. And yet of course this comfort – like the perfect home we tried to create – is, to put it mildly, an illusion.

From Washington, let me take you south by 600 miles or so to the state of South Carolina and to the city of Charleston, where the American South begins, where you can drive down Route 17 in the steamy heat, with the breeze all but non-existent, out of Charleston and down into the low country, the salt marshes. Charleston is one of America's most elegant cities, but Route 17 is not on any tourist maps, at least not as an attraction in its own right. In a sense, though, it should be. It gives a wonderful insight into hardscrabble American life, the sleazy glamour of the road that repels and appeals to visitors – and indeed Americans themselves – in roughly equal measure: gas stations, tattoo parlours, Bojangles Pizza, $59-a-night motels, pawn shops, gun shops, car showrooms, nail bars, and Piggly Wiggly, the local supermarket chain which, in my limited experience, smells almost as odd as it sounds. Piggly Wiggly, by the way, was one of your first contributions to world culture; it was the world's first supermarket. Mr Piggly and Mr Wiggly – I am guessing at the etymology but I may well be right – had the then revolutionary idea of abolishing the high counter that, in shops of yester-year, came between the shopper and the goods. It was a move that has affected the world as much as the invention of the light bulb or the washing machine, but Piggly Wiggly just don't seem too darn fussed. That's life in the South. That's life on Route 17 – stolid and ragged and smelling slightly of gasoline and chicken fried in motor oil.

It is a panorama of the mundane: Doric columns a-plenty but all of them made of cheap concrete and attached to restaurants or two-bit accountants' offices. On and on it goes, encroaching into the palm forests with no hint of apology.

The following morning I found myself standing next to a black four-wheel-drive vehicle and another quintessentially American phenomenon: a politician mired in Bible-laced hypocrisy.

At the time I met Mark Sanford, the then Governor of South Carolina whom I had made the journey to Charleston to meet and profile for the BBC, I didn't know about the hypocrisy. But I should have guessed when he offered to let me in on a secret. He was a closet tiller of fields, he said, and liked nothing better than to get out with his boys and work the land. He took me for a drive in his

Governor's limo and after a few minutes we slowed and took a turn down a lane that ended in a field. It was hot. Under a tree stood the Governor's tractor. The limo was parked, the clothes changed, and the Governor began ploughing. Up and down, up and down, through the heat haze. It was a wholesome picture that we duly shot for our profile.

In fact, it was a little too wholesome to be true. Weeks after telling me that all-American story, it emerged that Sanford was also ploughing furrows in foreign fields. The Governor disappeared for a few days, and was eventually tracked down to Buenos Aires, where he was found with an Argentine woman who was not Mrs Sanford, and with whom it transpired that he had been having a lengthy affair. This behaviour from a man so Christian and God-fearing that, when he was a congressman, he lived in some peculiar Christian fellowship house in DC. It did not stop his Doric columns from being false. He lost his job and with it the chance of vying to be the Republican presidential candidate in 2012. He was eaten alive by a public, half of whom were probably jealous of his Argentine adventure but all of whom no doubt attended those mean little churches that dot South Carolina, the signs outside them saying things like "Don't make me have to come down and sort you out: God!"

And yet for all the ugliness, the deadening tawdriness of much of the American landscape and the tinny feebleness of many of your politicians – the former Democratic Governor of Illinois who tried to sell Barack Obama's old Senate seat, or congressman Todd Akin who doesn't know how babies are made despite sitting on the House Science and Technology Committee – for all that nastiness and shallowness and flakiness, there is no question in my mind that to live in America was the greatest privilege of my life. We English still have much to learn from the way you have ploughed your furrows, with the mental equipment you took over to the New World. We can benefit from seeing ourselves now, in the modern age, through your eyes. And you can benefit from returning the compliment.

England's relationship with America – not Mr Cameron's relationship with Mr Obama, but truly *all of our* relationships with *all of you*; our understanding of your way of life and your grasp of ours – is important for two reasons. First, as Mitt Romney tried, albeit clumsily, to assert in his London trip before the 2012 election, our relationship is the cornerstone of the English-speaking world, which has so dominated the history of the globe in recent centuries and contributed enormously to the health, wealth and happiness of everyone. To accept this, you do not have to subscribe to the view that everything that the English-speaking world has done has been glorious and right, or that non-English-speaking peoples have contributed little to human progress; but the thrust of recent history has been provided by the people who brought you Magna Carta, the Glorious Revolution, the Declaration of Independence and the openness to innovation and democratisation that encouraged the greatest accumulation of wealth the world has ever seen. To an extent that torch was passed to the West with the *Mayflower*, but not entirely. Americans can still learn from Britain and still do. And we, too, can learn from you – not least, as *The Times* remarked in a wistful editorial after Barack Obama's visit to London in May 2011, in the area of self-confidence and assertiveness: we have lost our ability to trumpet our achievements and recognise our worth; you have not. The success of the London Olympics surprised nearly everyone in England. You are surprised by failure, not success.

Secondly, consider the claim that America belongs to us as much as to you. The immensity of America, its energy and zest for life, used to remind me sometimes of India. And like India, where I spent some time for the BBC many moons ago, America shines a light on the entire human condition. Few other nations really do. Italy reveals truths about Italians, Afghanistan about Afghans, Fiji about Fijians. But America speaks to the whole of humanity because the whole of humanity is represented there; our possibilities and our propensities. Often what is revealed is unpleasant; truths that are not attractive or wholesome or hopeful. On the last day we spent in our home in north-west Washington, a burger bar at the end of our street was holding an eating competition. The sight was nauseating: acne-ridden youths, several already obese, stuffing meat and buns into their mouths while local television reporters, the women in dinky pastel suits, rushed around getting the best shots. America can be seen as little more than an eating competition: a giant, gaudy, manic effort to stuff grease and gunge into already-sated innards. You could argue that the sub-prime mortgage crisis – the Ground Zero of the great recession and arguably an event or set of events more damaging than

9/11 – was caused mainly by greed: a lack of proportion, a lack of proper respect for the natural way of things that persuaded companies (encouraged by politicians) to stuff mortgages into the mouths of folks whose credit rating was always likely to induce an eventual spray of vomit.

There is an intellectual ugliness as well: a dark age lurking; a book-burning tendency never far from the surface of American life, even when the President has been to Harvard. For me this darkness was epitomised by the death in Wisconsin of a little girl who should still be alive. Eleven-year-old Kara Neumann was suffering from Type One diabetes, an auto-immune condition my son Sam also has. Her family, for religious reasons, decided not to take her to hospital when she fell ill. Instead, they prayed by her bedside and she died.

The night before she died – and she would have been in intense discomfort – her parents called the founder of a religious website and prayed with him over the telephone. But they did not call a doctor.

If Kara had been taken to hospital, even at that late stage, insulin could have saved her. She could have been home in a few days and chirpy by the end of the week, as my son was in the same situation. It was an entirely preventable death caused, let's be frank, by some of the Stone Age superstition that stalks the richest and most technologically advanced nation on earth. I deplore the superstition and the eating competitions and the tatty dreariness of so much of America, but I am convinced that these aspects of your country are not the flip side of its greatness, as some believe, but actually part of that greatness. You cannot have the good without the bad: there is something about the carelessness of America that gives space for greatness.

Out on Route 17 in South Carolina, you can do very well or very badly. You can crash and burn, or you can fill up with cheap gas (yes, folks, it really is still cheap to English eyes) and ride on into the sunset. If you do not like yourself in South Carolina, you can hire a self-drive truck and take it to Seattle. If you do not like your life and you have ambition and a little luck, you can change it because – being American – you believe you can change it. The reality is that American social mobility is stalled, but the myth still powers men and women and, if the stall can be broken, the dreams are still there to power revival.

My favourite story of American progress: sitting in a dingy New York apartment watching Perry Mason on the TV, Sonia Sotomayor, only eight-years-old and suffering from Type One diabetes, decided she was going to make it big in law. In 2009, by now in her fifties and having triumphed over poverty and daily insulin injections and the health scares that will have accompanied her condition, she was a Supreme Court Justice.

But if Sonia Sotomayor can make it big, there must be something creating the drive, and part of that something is the poverty of the alternative, the discomfort of the ordinary lives that most Americans endure and the freedom that Americans have to go to hell if they want to. This is what English people often fail to grasp about your nation. This is the atmosphere in which Nobel Prize-winners are nurtured. A nation that will one day mass-produce a cure for Type One diabetes could not – would not – save little Kara Neumann from the bovine idiocy of her religious parents.

And yet there is something missing. And that, to an extent, is where we English can help. America has lost sight, I think, of some of the subtleties of human life, some of the political compromises and mental accommodations that go towards making the good life on earth and are arguably part of the reason that English-speaking peoples have been as successful as they have. America is future-focused to be sure, and in many ways benefits from this attitude; but the place has become crazed by fights over fundamental world-views that actually do not matter very much. The Obama presidency coincided with, and to some extent caused, a fight to the death over culture that America really does not need to have. In the Britain of the coalition government we have battles about the here and now: the future is for folks to whom we have not been introduced and about whom we do not currently care. We still get drunk together, while sober Americans seethe and plot.

Having said that, this book is anything but a serious political text. It is intended as a snapshot of a rather odd moment in history, when the go-getters got their knickers in a twist, while the old country plodded on. A moment when the highly respected and serious-minded American political commentator David Brooks made a journey to Britain and found that, for the first time ever, he had left a pessimistic place and come east to a more optimistic one. Britain is phlegmatic and practical in the modern age; America is behaving like a middle-aged man in the grip of a full-scale mid-life crisis. America has gone out and bought a motorbike and is driving it too fast. Mr and Mrs America argue constantly – she thinks he is mad and he thinks she is dull and ugly. We look at you and we see you are in a mess. Even the killing of Osama bin Laden – an event of seismic political importance in the US, utterly underestimated in most English reporting – failed to do the trick. That provides an opportunity for Britons who like and admire America to rethink the relationship we should have with it in the future; to rethink the reality of both the ties that bind us and the utter separateness of some of our customs and heritage. So this is about you and us and, most importantly, the space between, which is filled sometimes with distrust and venom and sometimes with genuine communion of spirit.

It is about the special relationship. There: I have said it. The latest twist is that the relationship has become essential rather than special. And the White House now understands that while special was silly, essential is, well, essential. I doubt it. On my last day at the White House, I was thrown out of the study of a senior official when I mentioned the special relationship. "Gettoutahere!" he screamed. "You people are all mad." Obama folks felt, and feel, that they have more important things to focus on. They are right, probably, but that need not stop us thinking about these matters and coming up with a vision of you and us that genuinely accords with history and fits the times.

Chapter Two

Britain is a proud independent nation with a distinct
sense of our own values and traditions, many of which are
very sharply different, and, in some cases contradictory to
America's.
Peter Oborne, *Daily Telegraph*, May 2011

Forget Europe wholly, your veins throb with blood,
to which the dull current in her is but mud.
Let her sneer, let her say your experiment fails,
In her voice there's a tremble, e'en now while
She rails.
Robert Lowell, "A Fable for Critics"

ROBERT SOUTHEY, A traveller to America in 1809,
wrote that the people he saw possessed "a distinct
national character, and even a national physiognomy".

American heads were a different shape. He was right, I think.

The fact is that Americans believed long before most Britons did in democracy meaning the rule of all. To justify slavery, you convinced yourselves that slaves were fundamentally different. But all those inside the tent were to be treated as equals. There was no other way. Majority rule was invented in the US, not in the UK, and it shows. We reached bargains with our rulers on our side of the Atlantic but you owned your rulers, and your constitutional set-up, from the start. And you also believed from the outset in majority rule – or anyone's rule – being strictly limited. The Tudor polity you stole from England had all the trappings of English balance – with the king, the president, held in check. But you added to the brew a self-conscious unwillingness to allow any government to be high and mighty. You have never had, to use the English term of which we used to be oddly proud, "an elective dictatorship". Your tradition is anti-government in a way that really owes more to the taming of the prairies than to the small print of Magna Carta. One of the oddities of American history is why the welfare state – the habits and the theory of support for the poorest – never took off in the US. The reason for this is that alongside a belief in democracy, Americans maintained from the beginning a belief in self-help and individual betterment. As one nineteenth-century American magazine put it:

> Legislation has been the fruitful parent of nine-tenths of all the evils, moral and physical, by which mankind has been afflicted since the creation of the world, and by which human nature has been self degraded, fettered, and oppressed.

A thought: we English have never thought that. Not when kings ruled, not when parliamentary democracy was taking off, and not now when we are all in it together. We legislate to improve. Our tradition is utterly different. Look at the grief Lady Thatcher still gets for suggesting that society does not exist separately from families. Americans dislike government but when it has to exist they keep it close to them in their states or neighbourhoods. We rather like government; we enjoy being governed. We are way, way too busy to get involved. "Politicians are all the same," we say, meaning: let them get on with it because we have a bus to catch. We are so lazy! We have never really governed ourselves or shown any interest in it. We are happy for administrative classes to develop and flourish and decay and smell nasty and then be replaced by others – quasi-autonomous government organisations of people's peers. We have no pressure for term limits (a feature of American political debate) or sense of ownership of our tribunes. We don't like them any more than you like yours but we have no sense of ownership. The rhetoric, particularly after members of parliament were found to be fiddling their expenses on a grand scale, is about seizing the process, revivifying politics, getting involved. The reality, to my eyes, is that we don't really want to.

So our political closeness to you Americans is to some extent a sham. The British wit and writer of the 1930s, Philip Guedalla, used to say that any American ambassador to London had to use the meaningless term "glorious heritage" when describing any aspect of UK–US affairs – and stick very much to that heritage and history rather than modern issues or modern-day American achievements in any field: "in general it is undesirable that he should confess awareness of any author subsequent to the Declaration of The Independence!"

The ambassador could be rude – tread on toes, a sign of him being in the family – so that, in the words of Guedalla, "he ministers to the complete misunderstanding that is the sole safeguard against war between the US and UK".

The historian William Clark, writing in 1957, said: "The most significant fact about the development of Britain's attitude to America is that it began in humiliation which was later tempered by oblivion."

Oblivion! Those who prate about our closeness forget the historical evidence that for much of the time the United States has been alive we Brits have ignored it.

The Americans used to complain. Senator Lodge wrote to A. J. Balfour in 1896: "You have kept yourselves in a state of ignorance about the United States. Until very recently your newspapers gave it less space than to Belgium or Holland. Surely this was not wise." This American upset at a lack of proper recognition persisted for much longer than you might think. In 1953, the *New York Tribune*'s London correspondent wrote that press coverage in the UK was "altogether inadequate to enable British readers to follow the major events of the United States and express any intelligent opinions about them".

Could we, in fact, have been enemies? Might the English-speaking peoples have been fractured in a way that would make talk of mutual bonds of history look utterly hollow and false? We certainly fell out during the revolution and in the war of 1812, during which the British burned the White House to the ground. Throughout that period there was a nationalistic fervour in America that was decidedly anti-British, with a sense that the British were merely waiting for an opportunity to damage and destroy the upstart nation. And the upstart nation fought back – in particular with school textbooks that taught that Britain was a force for malignancy, not the wellspring of common values. William Clark writes of a visit to a Midwestern school in 1938, where he overheard a speech by a ten-year-old: "Britain owes us her national existence, which we saved in the last war; she owes us her empire which we fought to preserve; she owes us billions of dollars in war debts – and what do we get? Gratitude? No – insults!"

Throughout the nineteenth century, it is fair to say that Britain and America were really in the business of falling out more than celebrating the common bonds of heritage. The process was aided by the influx of anti-British Irish immigrants in the 1840s, but more than anything else, it was caused by the mishandling of the American Civil War, during which Britain managed to fall out with both sides. It was said at the time that a war with Britain was the only thing that could have united the armies of Grant for the North, and Lee for the South.

America was angry then for much of the nineteenth century and Britain was the focus. As Rudyard Kipling, who lived in America, put it: "England was still the dark and dreadful enemy to be feared and guarded against." And towards the end of the century, as America was getting powerful as well as angry, it was with Britain that it nearly went to war. The cause of this potentially history-altering spat was Venezuela.

The problem was a border dispute between British Guyana and Venezuela, a dispute given added zest by the presence of gold in the disputed area. The British still had the power to seize land anywhere in the world and the threat was clear: that they would put Venezuela in its place and by extension point out to the Americans the limits of their power and influence.

The Americans cited the Monroe Doctrine under which, according to them, no European power had the right to lord it over South America. This was the United States' backyard. The response from the British was imperious – Lord Salisbury, the Prime Minister, wrote a lecturing letter to the Americans, in which he airily pointed out that the Doctrine had not been accepted by Britain or indeed anyone else. High-handedness from a Lord! So British. And guaranteed down the ages to get the Americans upset.

A wave of patriotic fervour swept the United States and Congress was asked by the President to send its own commission to Venezuela with the power to adjudicate on the disputed land and enforce the outcome. The *New York Sun* carried the headline "War if Necessary!" and some even talked about taking Canada while they were about it. For a week it looked like war. Fratricidal or civil war, some said, but war nonetheless. In the end it did not happen, thanks at least in part to a sense in both nations that it would have been an odd and rather unseemly conflict – an absurdity as well as a crime, as Joseph Chamberlain called it – but still the fact remains that war was on the cards. No bond of friendship prevented the two nations from coming to the brink: indeed the opposite; the hostility that had simmered since the beginning could still be brought to the boil at any moment.

It was imperialism, not a love of democracy, that brought the United States and Britain together. The Americans, shortly after the Venezuela business was resolved, got the taste for foreign conflict and foreign dominion. It began over the Spanish possession of Cuba and the Philippines. After a nasty incident in Cuba, in which an American warship was blown up, the Americans and the Spanish went to war. The end result was Cuba's independence and – for the first time since the Declaration of Independence – American invasion and domination of a foreign nation: the Philippines. The history of America's Philippine venture could hardly be less glorious; it resulted in appalling suppression of local nationalists, in which many thousands of civilians were killed. It was an utter mess – one of those lessons of history that only historians seem to notice.

But at the time others *did* notice and drew rather fabulous conclusions about the significance of the Philippines to Anglo-American friendship. Finally the Yanks were showing themselves to be real men, or, to be more precise, real White Men.

Kipling, impressed as never before, wrote his famous poem "The White Man's Burden" as a direct response to the Spanish–American war. "Take up the White Man's Burden" was an exhortation aimed directly at the Americans. Kipling was not alone. A motley collection of Englishmen and Americans hoped that this was the moment to seize the initiative and – incredibly, given the history of the nineteenth century – to link our nations together once again.

Lord Cromer, for instance, excited by the temporary annexation of Cuba by the United States, declared his support because "I want the world to see that Anglo-Saxons can govern a decadent Latin race". Cromer was a former Consul General in Egypt and a believer in the White Man's Burden (and it was definitely "*Man's*" – he ended his days heading the National League for Opposing Woman Suffrage) but he was by no means a lone eccentric. Proposals were made for a union of greater Britain – Cecil Rhodes among those in the vanguard. There was to be an imperial federation of all English-speaking peoples. By the end of the century, the idea was attracting notable, if not widespread, support. In 1898, Joseph Chamberlain called for the Stars and Stripes and the Union Jack to wave together over an Anglo-Saxon alliance. The establishment of a colonial office in Washington was predicted. The imperial enthusiast Rhodes was agitating behind the scenes for what he called "the ultimate recovery of the United States as an integral part of the British Empire". To this end he proposed that there should be an imperial parliament that might sit for some time in London and for some in Washington.

As ever, Kipling found the words: "After a nation has pursued certain paths alone in the face of some slight misrepresentation, it is consoling to find another nation (which one can address without a dictionary) preparing to walk along the same lines to, I doubt not, the same ends."

The nation that once lowered the magazine postal rate to Canada to try to stop American cultural domination (take that, Hollywood) was now at least partly in love with the idea of a permanent union. Of course, in the end it came to nothing, and in the coming to nothing there was and is a message for those who preach that we and you are one. The lesson is: we are not one. Never were, since the inception.

The truth is that the colonists had grown apart from the old country long before they declared their independence, and nothing could ever or can ever bring us together. The American backers of the reunification of the English-speaking peoples, few in number, represented a strand in American politics rather than any kind of national feeling. The most prominent of these was probably the newspaper editor W. T. Stead. Stead wanted to "realize the great idea of race union" by merging the British Empire and the United States under essentially US control. Stead was no loony. He wrote convincingly and presciently about the domination of American culture and was one of the first to point out that its power lay (as it lies still) in its ability to seduce rather than in any forced adaptation. But Stead was not backed by supporters of a similar calibre. Rather, they were the *Mayflower* folk; upset at the swarm of Irish and Italian and other hyphenated Americans landing on America's shores. They were worried about race and colour and as such were somewhat un-American. They were the Lord Cromers of the United States, though in a much tinier minority than even the noble Lord was in Britain. Mitt Romney's advisers might have read a bit about them before using that unfortunate "Anglo-Saxons" line during the London visit in 2012.

It was never going to happen, this remarriage of the English-speaking peoples. Stead died on the *Titanic*, aptly enough. The First World War and the changes it brought to the balance of world power, and to thinking about imperialism and war and culture more generally, put paid to the remnants of the scheme, if a scheme it ever genuinely was. Randolph Bourne, now largely a forgotten figure but at the time of the First World War an important public intellectual, decided that "the good things in the American temperament and institutions were not English but were the fruit of our superior cosmopolitanism". Bourne wanted America to become – in the modern parlance – multicultural rather than a nation of settlers who sign on for the Anglo-Saxon world-view and self-view. He saw America teaching the British and the rest of the world a lesson. This vision of the role of the United States – as teacher and leader and exemplar – was held not only by the anti-war and anti-intervention Bourne but by writers and thinkers and politicians across the whole political spectrum. America came of age in the early part of the last century; the British and the Americans

spent the century before as enemies, came together
in the heads of the imperialists for a tiny sliver of
time at the dawn of the new age (the White House
flew flags at half-mast on the death of Queen Victoria
– a first), but then diverged suddenly and decisively
at around the time of the First World War. Political
union was not to be.

And soon the ignorance and dismissiveness at
the hands of the Brits that the Americans used to
complain of was very much a reverse phenomenon.
F. Scott Fitzgerald wrote after the war that the entire
continent of Europe was now "of merely antiquarian
interest". We had ignored you in the past and now
you were returning the favour. This was the beginning of American insouciance about the details of
the rest of the world, an insouciance that, to the
disappointment of some of his keener European
fans, did not die with the arrival of President Obama.
Far from it. I remember horror among the Brits
on the Obama press plane on his first trip to the
UK, shortly after becoming President. We opened
our White House briefings on the nation we were
visiting and discovered that the opening gambit, the
central fact about the dear old mother country, was
that it was "slightly smaller than Oregon"! And we

didn't really learn much more – some stuff about the Romans and modern-day friendship, but that was that. Oregon has a population of under four million and a contribution to the history of the world that is, it is fair to say, not yet worthy of much study. Lord Cromer would be revolving in his grave at the enormity of the snub. Now, to be fair to the White House, size does matter to Americans, because y'all have a hazy idea of the relative bulk of European states and after a night on a plane and arriving at London airport you need to be broken in gently. But even so, the land of Shakespeare and Milton and Wellington and Churchill reduced to this: *slightly smaller than Oregon*. Years before, I had been with President Bush on a visit to Belfast. The press pack then had referred to the destination as "Ireland". We were indeed on the island of Ireland, but did they not grasp that there was an important distinction – in fact, that that distinction was what all the fuss was about? From Bush to Obama and beyond; they do not really take our disputes seriously any more than they have respect for the size of our land mass. We are small and old and frail.

There are some Americans who cling to the Britishness of your culture, largely because they feel out of sorts with the people who have just moved into their neighbourhood. True political Americanism, as it were, is something alien to Britain. It is not – absolutely not – a kind of free-market, anything-goes attitude to life that some on the left equate with American values. It is more complex and nuanced than that – focused on limited government and extraordinary social energy, sometimes linked to government and sometimes not. But this energy and this zest for practical betterment and openness to talent is not British.

It hurts. The English-speaking peoples indeed. Robert Lowell's "blood and mud" jibe echoes down the years. History is on his side. Our political cultures are much less connected than we sometimes think and are becoming less connected by the day. At the end of the Obama visit to London in 2011, the English political commentator Peter Oborne was almost alone, but entirely right, in my view, in suggesting that the treatment of the President had verged on the sycophantic: sinister, he called it. Oborne pointed out that when the relationship between our nations really was special – or essential – there had been no need for all the flummery of a state visit. No post-war president had been granted one until George W. Bush. None had needed one, perhaps, nor this pretence that you and we are hewn from the same political and social rock. There is a foolishness – a brittle quality – to our modern-day efforts to claim we are all on the same page, all the time. We are not. And we never have been.

Chapter Three

THE FALL HAS proved the strangest, most discom-
bobulating time of year for a family settling back
into English life. By the time our second autumn
came along, we were beginning to feel confident
once again with the hallmarks of Englishness: the
price of petrol as we now remembered to call it, the
sense of irony, the mists and mellow fruitfulness. All
was going swimmingly. Until we were knocked off
balance by the trees.

Fall colours – colors, to be accurate – are one of
the great joys of American life. You do not get them
anywhere else. This is your American conceit and
we believed it with the passion of all immigrants
to the New World. As the United States National
Arboretum website has it: "In areas that are often
cloudy for much of the autumn, with rather warm
temperatures, fall colors are dull at best. This is often
the case in much of Europe."

Ouch. That puts us in our place. The ideal conditions for brilliant autumn colours are a warm, wet spring combined with a sunny, cool autumn. We often have the former on our side of the pond but the judgement is correct: we rarely enjoy the latter. You have these conditions – especially in New England but also extending down south into Virginia – almost every year. The result is breathtaking; in particular, I always felt, when savoured alongside that other great American vista: the sleazy glamour of the road I mentioned in the introduction, the glamour that both repels and appeals to visitors – and indeed Americans themselves – in roughly equal measure.

America, as you know, can be pretty ugly. The tat! And then turn a corner and your jaw will drop. A panorama of the mundane gives way to America's greatest asset: its space and its natural beauty.

The colours of the American autumn, the coppers, the yellows, the deep reds and purples, stretch in some states for as far as the eye can see. America has always, right from the beginning, been a land of trees. The American historian James Harmon McElroy suggested that the taming of the forest and the wilderness has been the principal event in the history of the American people; everything else has flowed from this struggle to preserve nature but to conquer it as well.

Now this is where our autumn colours come in. Shortly after returning to England we had an autumn of American grandeur. Walking on the hills outside the beautiful West Country city of Bath, we were shocked as a family to see sights that we thought we had left behind for ever. A genuine New England vista in old England. The whole marvellous copper-tinged, yellow-flecked gorgeousness laid out before us, with the city of Bath thrown in for good measure.

It was a surprise, this view, and that, it occurred to us later, was itself an added bonus. Because one of the great ironies of American life is that along with the space and the freedom and the sense of rugged adventure that living there can bring – the fact that American woods really do have bears in them and American weather can kill with its hurricanes and tornadoes and apocalyptic electrical storms – there is also in the American psyche a desire, as James Harmon McElroy suggests, to tame all of this wildness.

So the American fall colours are often experienced in a dispiritingly regimented way. The trip from

Washington DC to the absolutely stunning Skyline Drive is a case in point. This road runs for a hundred miles along the crest of the Blue Ridge Mountains in Shenandoah National Park. It is breathtaking because the crest really is a crest: the hills fall away and the vistas on both sides are huge and unspoiled. But it's gated! You cannot get onto the road without going past a little lodge and paying a toll. And once you've paid and are on the road, there is no stopping except at designated vista points. There is no walking unless you keep to the paths, and each one has been thoughtfully graded for you in advance so that you can judge whether Granny or the kids will survive this brush with nature.

In other parts of the country, there are entire websites devoted to telling you which autumnal colour will be where and for how long. They have turned autumn into an industry. It is the American way.

So we, in England, should doubly celebrate our autumns when they burst into life and shock us all. First, because they provide an explosion of colour and a reminder that even in our crowded nation, with its mild and uninteresting weather, we can manage beauty that competes with anywhere else on earth. And then, for the joy of the surprise. You can boast of how dependable your fall can be but its very dependability dulls the colour, as it were; real vibrancy is unforced, unexpected, untrammelled by rules and regulations and guides to the best views and the gentlest paths. Life in England is more colourful than I remembered. More than ever, after that walk near Bath, I was glad to be back.

And yet, when one tries to put one's finger on the reasons for our different approaches to such matters, the task is oddly difficult. What are the psychological drivers of America's desire to impose order? Does it really all come from the challenge of those vast forests that greeted the first settlers? Is there an atavistic need to fight off bears that makes you Americans what you are? And the same questions can be asked of the British: why are we so bloody relaxed about everything? Why do we stumble upon autumn colours and have no need to be told where to go and what to do?

So here is another area in which we can help you Americans refind your better selves and in doing so refind the kind of mental capacity that led to the successes of your past. We have to help you with your failure to see the wood for the trees. For you have become so sclerotic in your habits that you have lost the flexibility to act in your own best interest: inventing Google but falling behind in maths education; inventing Google but failing to notice that the world is networked and traditional power structures outdated; inventing Google but not noticing that you invented Google.

The real issue here is whether America can be persuaded to do what is necessary to continue to lead in a changed world. You need to be persuaded that you have the capacity and the social structure that could render all the talk of Chinese and Indian dominance premature, if not utterly redundant. I think it can be done. And it begins with demographics. America is small and young. You are not used to seeing it in those terms but it is the truth. Its population burst through 300 million – to much celebration – in 2006 and will get to 400 million in the next few decades, but these numbers are modest and manageable when set against the actual and potential populations of India and China. Those nations have to cope with territorial and ethnic divisions and political structures that take note of those divisions without allowing them to become dominant drivers in local politics. America does not have these problems. There is nothing fissiparous about the US (alright, the Alaskans have muttered about independence but they are, as we will see later, deluded) and there is a cultural myth to which most Americans subscribe. *Ça marche!* Will China? Will India?

I was struck by the sight of the Chinese Olympics opening ceremony in 2008. In so many respects the games were a showcase for the new Asian century. They were spectacular and well organised and stunning. And yet when you looked at the opening ceremony – the parade of teams through the main hall – the weakness of so much of the world was also on show. All those athletes who looked so completely as you expected them to. The Italians, the Congolese, the Russians and, of course, more than anything, the Indians and the Chinese. They were ethnically and socially similar; representing nations nervous about interconnectivity. Then in came the Americans. Madness! A great seething mass of humanity with every look and every background on show. Americans from Africa, Americans from Asia, Americans from Europe, Americans from the Middle East, Americans from Mars and Venus and all points in between. Throughout history, this ability to attract talent and cope with influxes of humanity has been part of the American way, but now there is a special relevance to it.

This century is the century of the network. It is the Wikicentury. Terrorists use them and governments use them but so do universities and societies and companies and individuals. The nation state has not withered away but it has been overtaken in many important ways by those who can connect with each other, share ideas and share experiences, innovate and re-create in an atmosphere of genuine freedom, a culture that respects troublesome views as much as it respects conformity. America used to be good at this and could be good at it again. You can have any number of science parks – Chinese style – but if you do not have the freedom to chat on the internet about what you are discovering and what implications it might have, you miss out on the real driving force of the future: being at the hub of the network. To be there requires a culture, political and social, that values people who speak their mind. It also needs to value truth as best we know it – scientific truth, which is always open to challenge. This is why America's broadcasting set-up, I believe, needs to take a long, hard look at whether it encourages shouting at the expense of anything like proper freedom for competing ideas to be understood and evaluated.

There is a wonderful book by Robert Wright called *Non Zero: the Logic of Human Destiny*. It was published before 9/11, so became a bit crowded out by military matters and the struggle for the immediate future of human destiny. But in the longer term the ideas in this book need to be looked at again. Wright suggests that history is – contrary to the fashion these days – a story of the evolution and improvement of humankind. The fundamental improvement is the realisation that life need not be zero-sum: in other words, my gain need not be your loss. We can both gain, from trade, from friendship, from the sharing of art. The biggest benefits, if Wright is right, will accrue to those nations who can be in a position to gain in the future because they are in the centre of the hub, open culturally, physically and mentally to all that everyone has to say.

This is not an argument that the internet solves everything. The net can be used by authoritarian powers and can be a tool of social control. But if a nation can position itself as genuinely open to ideas and genuinely chatty in the connected world, then it has a mighty advantage.

It is really about creative tension and creative energy. It is about using information as power on a truly global stage. It is about government power to act quickly because the kind of information that used to be provided – unreliably – by spies and satellites is increasingly going to be there for the taking if only you have the eyes to see and the linguistic and intellectual skills to use the knowledge when it comes. It is about the power of commercial interests to seize opportunities before competitors even know the opportunities are there. It is about the power of individuals to cross borders without passports. Will all this happen in China and India? Could it?

The point is that America is in a position to achieve continuing power and influence (authority is perhaps the better word) through giving up on hegemony. We have to help you by persuading US politicians that they have to be blunt with the American people: power in the future will not come through the kind of dominance represented by all those US military bases that dot the globe. In fact, most of them can close. Power will come from an understanding that human diversity is to be celebrated and ideas and divergences of opinion and solutions that begin as eccentric and eventually become mainstream must all be encouraged. When you look at Chinese success in industrialisation it is very difficult to argue that democracy and chaos might have made it even more successful – chances are it would not, and democracy did not exist in England when we led the way with the world's first industrial revolution either. But when industrialisation turns into real modernity then the need for the structures of free society become more obvious. And that is where America could still have an edge over China that lasts at least for the rest of this century, an edge that confounds those who predict China's rise and America's decline.

The problem for America is getting there. The temptations not to do so – to instead focus on old allies (London and Washington or Paris and Washington) – are real and ever present. But the prize for all of us if America breaks free is incalculable: a world in which the dominant force is progressive and humane, focused on medical advance rather than religious conformity, on problem-solving rather than blame-fixing, on the rights of existing individuals rather than future glory; that is the true prize.

America has to be persuaded to go back to the forests and the fall colours and just let them be. It has to go back to being surprised and energised. It has to abandon its gated communities. It has to maintain an immigration policy that encourages entry wherever possible. It has, in particular, to focus on the South American nations and the potential that they have in the future to build a powerbase of trade and innovation. If Mexico was rich and stable, how much better off would all Americans be? If Brazil were to be a serious diplomatic ally, how much more powerful would American ideas be in the future, than if America looks to London for the kind of unquestioning but resentful and half-hearted support it's all too often had in the past? Should America move to kick Britain off the UN Security Council? In public, this is not for serious consideration; in private, the thought is there and the reason – realistic appraisal of the future benefits that might accrue to the world – might not be antithetical to British interests. We have to allow you to get there.

We should set you free. You'll do yourselves – and in the process, us – a power of good.

Chapter Four

The land was ours before we were the land's.
She was our land more than a hundred years
Before we were her people. She was ours
In Massachusetts, in Virginia,
But we were England's, still colonials,
Possessing what we still were unpossessed by,
Possessed by what we now no more possessed.
Something we were withholding made us weak
Until we found out that it was ourselves
We were withholding from our land of living,
And forthwith found salvation in surrender.
Such as we were we gave ourselves outright
(The deed of gift was many deeds of war)
To the land vaguely realizing westward,
But still unstoried, artless, unenhanced,
Such as she was, such as she will become.
"The Gift Outright" by Robert Frost, read at the inauguration
of John Kennedy, 1961

"I CAN'T BELIEVE this place."

The speaker is my wife, Sarah, who from day one of our US adventure was a fan, an enthusiastic settler, but whose frustration on this occasion has boiled over. It's four in the morning and we have just been woken by what felt like a huge explosion; the kind of disruption of the Washington suburbs of which Osama bin Laden must have dreamed. But it wasn't him. An inspection reveals the cause of the bang and some buzzing aftershocks was an electrical power junction precariously placed on top of a pole under a large tree. In torrential rain and high winds, bits of the tree appear to have shorted the wires. The only time I have seen similar electrical arrangements was in the black South African township of Soweto outside Johannesburg during the days of apartheid, where the locals used to hook up their own wires to the junction boxes in order to enjoy free power from their white oppressors. In the rain, these unofficial electrical contrivances would look rather pretty as they fizzed and sparked, but I don't think anyone ever claimed they were particularly safe, and it was a surprise to find not dissimilar sights in the capital of the wealthiest nation on earth.

But America is eight parts rich, industrialised superpower and two parts cowboy frontier town. There is a rough edge to life here that separates the US from other wealthy places. As my then seven-year-old son Sam put it, shortly after we had returned from a camping trip in West Virginia, "America is rich, right? But it doesn't look it."

It doesn't look it for a whole host of reasons – many of them linked to geography: to the open spaces and the danger that lurks in them or passes over them, or even, on occasion, lies in wait under them. Being American you will know that there are bears in American woods: not many, perhaps a few thousand compared to the 50,000 there probably were before the white settlers arrived, but still enough to get the occasional human attacked and killed, enough to make camping in the American West a different experience from camping in, say, Devon in southern England. And here is the crucial point: enough to make America similar in some respects to nations that on the face of it could hardly be more different. I read some years ago that the deputy mayor of the Indian capital Delhi had been killed by a horde of wild monkeys, which had attacked him outside his home. To an English eye, the wildness of parts of

Delhi is strikingly alien; to an American, less so. To my knowledge, monkey attacks are rare in the US and attacks involving any wild animals in cities are almost unheard of, but the fact is that the idea of a wild creature coming across a human and doing him harm is not out of the way in the American psyche. It could happen; in reasonably recent memory, it used to happen a lot. When we Europeans look at you and your habits and customs and lifestyles, we need to remember this – to celebrate the fact that you really are different and this is one of the foundations of that difference.

But wild animals are only a minor issue compared with the meteorological and geophysical threats with which you Americans have to cope. In our first year in Washington we had two small tornados; a hurricane which uprooted thousands of trees, damaged hundreds of houses and left us without electricity for a week; an earthquake (4.5 on the Richter scale); a plague of tree-eating cicadas; snow; intense body-sapping humid heat; and countless more minor natural disturbances. No wonder Americans are a bit rough round the edges – you need to be. Even in your capital city, a place many Americans regard as effete to the point of girliness. This nation is a tough neighbourhood. And the natural environment has helped to mould a political and social culture which – for better or for worse – can seem unpolished to the European eye. Life is not as precarious as it was for the Pilgrim Fathers or indeed the Native Americans who already lived here, but a measure of the harshness they faced is still very much a part of local American experience. You need to point that out and those who cover America for European news organisations need to repeat it. There are no hurricanes in Europe. No tornados. The heat is less intense and less sapping. The cold is less bone numbing. The Venus and Mars distinctions that are sometimes made between Americans and Europeans do not simply spring from nowhere. They are rooted in geography.

The physical dangers first: America doesn't look rich because much of this nation is really hanging on to its place in the first world, battling against furious and ever-present opposition from Mother Nature. I had a friend who was an airline pilot in Europe; his biggest ambition was to move to the US because, as he put it, "the weather is more interesting". Frequent fliers here will readily confirm that fact, though they find it less compelling as a reason to live on your side of the Atlantic. The fact is that America's natural environment can be very interesting. It kills people, sometimes in large numbers. Tornado shelters are a feature of the Midwest; you think little of them in rural areas where everything still looks like the set from *The Wizard of Oz* (before it gets psychedelic), but when you see them in more up-to-date settings, in the shining steel structure of Denver Airport, for instance, you realise that nature here is untamed and untameable. The author Antonya Nelson has written of her native Kansas:

> In the centre of the country, the Kansan is aware of the vast span of time and space just outside the window. The world out there that insists an individual is just too tiny… to matter in the least.

True, Kansans live at the epicentre of America's tornado activity and there are plenty of Americans who have never seen a shelter, let alone had to rush to one, but this land is still their land. You have built your nation in the teeth of a storm. And the storm is never quite over. This was a recent item in a local newspaper, hardly more than filler:

> A blinding sandstorm that caught drivers by surprise

caused a 12-car pileup Tuesday on a highway in the high desert north of Los Angeles, killing at least two people and injuring 16.

A lunchtime sandstorm that reduced visibility to zero – interesting weather.

And after these storms, the natural environment is always able to cover its tracks and ours; the adventurer Steve Fossett disappeared in 2007 in a small plane over the desert in Nevada. Disappeared! They didn't find him and they gave up looking, though while the search was still on they found several other wrecks they didn't even know about. His turned up a full year later: some wreckage and some bones. This would not happen in Somerset. So forget for a moment that San Francisco sleeps every night, perched on a faultline which could lead at any moment to a catastrophic earthquake. Put Hurricane Katrina to one side. In fact, disregard all the recent news of large-scale geological and meteorological threats and potential threats. In daily life, in large swathes of America, people still look at the sky and wonder.

What you do not realise when you wonder is the extent to which that separates you from us. In the rest of the advanced world, by and large, they don't have to wonder. We certainly don't in England, where the twentieth anniversary of the great storm of 1987 was celebrated with special TV programmes and reminiscences from those involved. A brush with the weather was all it was – a weak hurricane and a chance to bash a weather forecaster called Michael Fish. Another brush with the weather – the great snow of 2009 – closed London and caused such excitement on the BBC News Channel that they brought Mr Fish back in to talk about it. That same week, 50 people died in ice storms in the American Midwest. You have to be made of sterner stuff.

And that is the point. Before I lived there, I could never quite understand why Americans seemed so coarse, so untouched by the civilisation I took for granted at home. How could they accept practices like execution, or long prison sentences for minor crimes, or gun ownership or indeed war, all of them things sophisticated Europeans have more or less left behind?

The best part of a decade spent among you lifted the scales from my eyes. I get it now, and we all could, if we would only focus on the causes of the harshness of American practices and the American way. The weather I have mentioned. When it comes to American disregard for the outside world, to that famous American ignorance about where Pakistan is on a map, or whether the United Kingdom is a Gulf Arab nation, size also matters. It really is a very long way from sea to shining sea. Even Americans get confused about the extent of their dominion: a magazine in New Mexico used to publish a regular feature entitled "one of our 50 is missing!" Readers would send in examples of organisations in other states wondering where exactly New Mexico might be and occasionally asking about the need for visas.

But ignorance of your own country is one thing; again and again anti-Americans complain about the attitude of Americans towards the rest of the world, about the insularity of American life, about the percentage of Americans who have passports or have been to Vladivostok or speak fluent Swahili. Yet outsiders – particularly Europeans – often have only the vaguest idea of where Kansas is, or Rhode Island, or indeed New Mexico. And how many British people – proud owners of passports – actually use them only to travel to France or Spain, the equivalent of a jaunt from Chicago to South Carolina, to get some sun and pop home? Americans don't need passports (until recently they didn't need them to go abroad either to Canada or the Caribbean). That is why they don't have them. To use the passport argument to suggest that Europeans are somehow keener explorers of the world is simply wrong. Of course, plenty of us are woefully ignorant of our fellow human beings, but the ignorance of Americans is held up as evidence of their hopeless inadequacy, while the rest of us are free to see the United States as New York, San Francisco and a blur of nameless places in between. It is like the difference between knowledge of the humanities and knowledge of applied science. You can be ignorant about how a light bulb works but still cut it in polite society if you know what Proust was getting at. Similarly, among the sophisticates of the world, a knowledge of the geography of Europe (where is Lichtenstein?) counts for a lot more than equivalent knowledge about the United States. Where is Nebraska? Don't care.

Should care, I say. But why? Well, as with the weather and the geology, American space gives clues about the formation of the American character. These are not get-out-of-jail cards for badly behaved presidents (Oh, you'll have to forgive him, he's from Texas, or pretends to be) but they are pointers towards greater knowledge of the American soul. We bend over backwards to know why "the Arab street" thinks as it does; in the case of America we should be equally curious to look for causes, wellsprings, beginnings. Our relationship with you should grasp this: it would be part of the process of coming to terms with the fact that you are different from us. When we expect you to be the same as us we make a foolish mistake, but worse than that we fail to ask the questions that might reveal why you are different. It is not a clever or sensible way of approaching a nation with whom we pretend to have so much in common.

> So luxuriant was the growth of the ten thousand year old forest that covered all but a few scattered portions of it – a forest that had developed after the retreat of the last Ice Age in North America – that mariners coming from Europe in the late spring or early summer were greeted while still at sea, far from the sight of land, by the mingled scent of sun-warmed resins from millions of pines and cedars and fragrance of myriad flowering shrubs and trees.

John Harmon McElroy, in his book *American Beliefs*, sets a scene that takes the breath away. It certainly gave pause to the early settlers, and, as I note later on, some of them pronounced such fecundity a touch overwhelming and probably not desperately conducive to civilised life. And it is true that for European gentlefolk it was not an easy place to live, this Stone Age vastness, this interminable and sometimes hostile wilderness. Many of the early European settlers starved because they simply could not put the place to work. But in time they managed, and managed hugely well. America's story has been the story of the conquest of the continent. As McElroy puts it:

> The continuous transformation of the great wilderness of forest, prairie, plains, mountains, and desert that once stretched across the entire centre of the world's third largest continent... has been the principal event in the history of the American people. The behaviours and consequences associated with that transformation have, directly and indirectly, shaped many of the beliefs of American culture.

It is worth adding that modern scholarship has convincingly overridden the idea that "the great wilderness" was entirely empty of people and, more crucially, of civilisation. A convincing case can be made – and is explored in Charles C. Mann's *1491* – that some of the rugged individualism of the American character comes directly from the organisation and social mores of Native American society, in particular from the loose confederacy of tribes and nations making up the Haudenosaunee ("People Building a Long House") who had successfully put an end to Stone Age tribal warfare long before the white men arrived. And in doing so had begun some of the traditions of which modern America is so proud. Mann quotes a seventeenth-century Jesuit complaining: "All these barbarians have the law of wild asses – they are born, live, and die in liberty without restraint; they do not know what is meant by bridle and bit".

Indeed. And many early settlers went off to live in these attractive conditions or lived so close to them that they became infected – particularly with what appears to have been the Indian lack of respect for social class and inherited authority.

But Native Americans and settlers alike had to do battle with the elements, with nature. This fight has left its mark. There is a strong belief, even in the modern nation, in the duty of all Americans to grapple with nature. The people who starved when they arrived here in the early seventeenth century tended to be the nobility. A belief in the almost sacred value of hard work, and of the rights of families to profit from hard work, surely began in those early frightening, coruscating winters. The earliest settlers brought with them the mores and practices of the Old World, of course, in particular the idea of indentured servitude, where a person had to "pay off" the cost of the passage with years of free labour. But even these people were soon better off than they had been at home. The per capita income of Americans in the years before the revolution was already higher than that of English people. America had already taken off before 1776. It had taken only a few years for the early settlers to realise that private property, widely owned, encouraged industry. Europeans, with their feudal system and the cultural baggage that surrounded it, with their tightly monitored villages and their strict hierarchies, had taken twenty times as long to civilise their continent. Some Europeans still don't get it.

But the driving force behind this American approach was not, and is not, some abstract academic belief in individualism. The idea that birth rank was irrelevant, that dukes were a joke if they could not till fields, that aristocratic titles were cute and fascinating but not directly relevant to everyday life, that social order needed to be efficient and conducive to maximum production and use of talents: they did not read this stuff in a book, or at least not until Milton Friedman arrived on the scene. American individualism springs directly from the need of the early Americans – including Native Americans – to survive and prosper and do it quickly. They chose what worked, in terms of social organisation and overarching ethic: hard work, everyone involved, and everyone able to benefit. They had space to parcel up and hand out, and that of course meant that huge numbers of ordinary people could own land; it also meant in time that millions of ordinary people were not part of a huge pool of labour for hire. Labour was expensive and wages were high.

The abundance of land also meant that people could avoid even the relatively light touch of authority in American townships and settlements; there was nobody to supervise you, no nobleman to respect, no church you were forced to join, no rigid structure holding you back. The result was a mental freedom, caused and sustained by the geography, which continues to this day.

The geography of America, and the opportunities and risks faced by the early settlers, is also responsible, I think, for the stunning, the unique, the shining example of American giving. Americans are the most generous people on earth. You give staggering sums of money: $229 billion was donated by individuals in 2007 according to Giving USA, an organisation that monitors charity and the charitable sector. Is this simple altruism? No, of course it isn't. Those American settlers who forged ahead into the wilderness all those years ago were wonderfully free but also horribly unprotected. They had to look after themselves and they had to collaborate with each other to do it; they learned the value of individualism and the cost of isolationism all wrapped up in one lesson. So they gave their time and their money for the common good. Unprotected by government, they sorted out their own solutions. And they still do. So American giving is often giving aimed at oneself and one's family. Even such limited generosity is something we Brits find culturally alien. An example: there is an American private school I have been told about, a multinational place outside which the flags of the various nationalities in attendance proudly hang. Save one. The Union Jack is not there. British children attend the school. British mums and dads pick them up and drop them off. But there is no flag. Why not? Well, the parents are meant to pay. The school will arrange to buy the flag but the parents must cough up the funds. The British parents, being British, think they pay plenty in fees already and have no desire to come up with the cash. Americans are horrified by this. I told the story once and an American in the audience (he was a cameraman, not poor but not super-rich) came up to me afterwards with a cheque book and offered to donate the requisite sum. The point is that Americans believe in self-help. You believe in charitable giving to prop up the comforts of everyday life. You give huge sums to foreign charities, it is true, and to disaster relief at home and abroad, but most of the cash is going towards the enrichment of your own existences.

On March 25th, 1745, ten men executed pledges totalling £185 "for the purpose of Erecting a Collegiate School in the province of New Jersey for the instructing of youth in the Learned Languages, Liberal Arts, and Sciences". Today, Princeton University's endowment is worth $14 billion. No British university, however much more ancient and venerable, can come close. And that money has been given, in the most part, by grateful former students. Students who feel themselves to be part of a private community just as their forebears did. De Tocqueville noticed it: in France and England he wrote, associations were formed generally from the top down – governments or "upper-class" people would organise them and run them and sustain them. In eighteenth-century America, however, "Americans of all ages, all conditions, all dispositions constantly form associations". They still do: and the reason they do, and the reason they fund them as well as they do, is again not the result of some academic commitment to the free market and charity as opposed to socialism and state dependency. The reason is to be found in the geography, in the need for self-reliance tempered by social responsibility that the early settlers grappled with and grasped. When President Obama tries to persuade Americans to volunteer and take part in their communities and their lives, he pushes on an open door, a door opened by history but more importantly by geography. When it was first inhabited the space was ungovernable in the old-fashioned sense: new forms of association and new ways of thinking were necessary for the great experiment to take flight.

There is still space in the US. Room to run. And I am not talking about the Great Plains. Ten minutes outside Washington DC – really, ten minutes – you can be in a wilderness overlooking the Potomac River with not a house, not a human being in sight. This is not the case in London or Paris or Rome or Berlin. And if you fall into the Potomac, into the rushing water at Great Falls, for instance, just a few minutes' drive out of DC, you are on your own. As you drown, you would see the airliners dipping down overhead to land at Reagan National Airport. You would know that you were very close to the levers of US power and the monuments to US might. But you would die nonetheless. America's physical environment breeds rugged individualism – the longer I lived in the US, the more I saw a causal link between the width of the place, its extent and its topography, and its mindset. Part of it is atavistic: or at least grounded in the experience of the early settlers who became landowners and land tamers on a scale never before seen in human history. But it is a mistake to assume that modern America – comfortable, slothful, suburban America – is so hugely different. Access to wilderness is not limited, as it is in Britain, to country folk or those who can afford a second home in the Lake District – cheap petrol (by European standards) and plenty of space combine to make this a nation of amateur explorers, conquerors of nature. You can load up the truck and ship out of town, any American town, and be lost before dusk. And when you get there you can get wild.

An example: I am in an opencast coal mine in West Virginia, the guest of a private mine owner who wants to publicise the benefits of coal as the fuel of the future. The chief benefit, truth be told, is that there is plenty of it left in the ground. This being a land of efficiency as well as a land of space, the mine owners take a very direct route to the seams of potential fuel: they blow the tops off the mountains. Europeans will shudder at the environmental wantonness of this activity (and many Americans do as well) but it does bring home to you the fact that this nation is chock-full of mountains, and the loss of a few peaks hardly registers on the national radar. I am musing on this point – and pulling on some boots for the hike around what's left of this particular mountain – when I notice something unnerving: several of the drivers of those super-sized mechanical diggers they favour in the macho world of the opencast pit are packing heat. The truck drivers have large guns – hunting rifles – pointing out of their cabs; they look like extras in some dark post-nuclear drama. In fact, the men are hunters enjoying the first day of the deer season – the mine owner improved morale by allowing his employees to take pot shots from their vehicles before they knocked off for the day. It's all very brutal – very dangerous – but here's the deal in the land of the free: if it is on private land, you can get away with it. You have to wear a red vest so that your buddy doesn't wing you but that appears to be the only rule.

What I witnessed in West Virginia was the coming together of two important traditions. First, that ordinary men (and women, I suppose, though not in West Virginia) have the right to carry weapons and kill animals – hunting in America is not the preserve of sherry-quaffing posh folk. Secondly, that on private property you can do your thing. An Englishman's home is his castle, we Brits used to say, but always in the knowledge that the castle was usually small, overlooked and surrounded by security cameras. In West Virginia, homes are often far from being castles. Often homes are trailers parked by the side of the road. But around them they have what the best castles have always had: plenty of space. Space to go crazy and kill animals.

Space as well to enslave and harm fellow human beings in a manner unimaginable in rural Yorkshire.

The brutal truth is that in this area – geofreedom – as in others of American life, there is a cost. And sometimes the cost is high. In 2008, a polygamous sect – an offshoot of the Mormon Church – was accused of practices that amounted to organised child abuse. In their Texas hideaway, on private land unseen by the forces of authority, it was alleged that they organised "marriages" between elderly men and girls as young as sixteen, marriages that were then "consummated" in front of other men. Someone complained to the police, who finally raided the compound. The children, amid scenes of great hand-wringing, were taken into protective custody. In the end, though, the evidence did not stand up and the children were returned.

But hold on. The sect belongs to Warren Jeffs, who is serving two consecutive prison sentences for being an accomplice to the rape of a fourteen-year-old girl who was married to her cousin in Utah. In spite of the fact that the leader of the sect is plainly a child abuser, the Texas authorities held back from investigating and are now in trouble (accused of unconstitutional behaviour) for going in when they did. This community had legally bought the land on which they planted their temple. No outsider complained about them. That is geofreedom.

Which is not to say that you always, or even commonly, use your space for brutal and destructive pursuits. Panoramic vistas mostly enhance American life and American attitudes. And the vistas boggle the mind. Monument Valley, that quintessential cowboy-film moonscape somewhere east of the Grand Canyon in the states of Arizona and Utah, ought to be one of the great tourist destinations of the world. It is unique – the red rocks that formed the backdrop to a hundred Western films and for the iconic advertising campaign of the Marlboro Man simply do not exist in this form anywhere else on the planet. For as far as the eye can see there is nothing but baked-sand desert and the huge protu-berances that ancient rivers have left standing in massive weird isolation. It is a view that stays with you for ever. But there is nobody there! Well, alright, in the height of the season there are cars on Route 163, the road that meanders past the monuments, but this is no Stonehenge. For one thing, it takes real determination to get to Monument Valley – it's a day's drive from Phoenix in Arizona or Santa Fe in New Mexico. And for another, there is just so much of it – hours and hours of space – that you never feel hemmed in. What does this do to the American soul? How does it affect the emerging folk memory of the American people? Does it speak of possibilities rather than limitations? Does it suggest exploration and adventure, over societal values of coexistence and self-control? Does it lead to an attitude of mind that squints at the horizon? Did the young Barack Obama do exactly that when his mum took him on a tour of the nation by Greyhound bus?

It is certainly true that many of America's finest hours, as seen by Americans, involve the conquest of natural obstacles. You are still at it, particularly out west, where a new population explosion is under way, in cities like Phoenix and Las Vegas. Vegas is, of course, uniquely odd; Phoenix has pretensions to being just a normal big city.

But look at it from the air: it really should not be there. All around is the parched desert of the south-west United States – the temperature outside the cocoon of air-conditioning is regularly over 40C. But the citizens are cool and Phoenix is expanding. It is an expensively hydrated testament to modern America's can-do spirit. Yet it exists on a knife edge. Modern Americans gave Phoenix its name because it seemed to be rising from the ashes of a past civilisation – the Hohokam people who lived there from early times, finally dying out in the fifteenth century. The author Craig Childs has written of the fate that may await modern-day Phoenix:

> When archaeologists study the Hohokam, they see a civilization that finally collapsed under the weight of drought, overpopulation, and ensuing social disarray. When they look at Phoenix, they see potential for the same.

Now I know that the UK could in theory suffer a similar fate. Global warming could bring searing heat to Weston-super-Mare. Birmingham could... Well, something could happen to Birmingham. But Americans, for all your bluster, and for all our visions of you as over-mighty conquerors of this, that and the other, still face dangers that we do not. My parents-in-law live in Reading, in Berkshire. Reading changes over the years; employment opportunities come and go, housing estates are built and expand, inner-city warehouses are done up and sold off, but none of these changes is driven by geography. Reading is where it is because three rivers meet there, but that geographical fact is no longer a driving force. There is a fetid stability in the English Home Counties that American towns do not have. In the US the towns themselves are every bit as stable – and often far uglier – but the hugeness of the nation that surrounds them invests American small-town life with a kind of edginess that most of the UK, most of Europe, cannot match.

The point of that Robert Frost poem is that Americans became American when they embraced the land: "such as we were we gave ourselves outright". Other nations grow organically over time; they are plainly shaped by the environment, but the impact is hidden or diluted by other inputs. In America the looming large of the land is a recent folk memory. Of course there is space in other nations, bad weather too, and all manner of natural hazards and propensity to calamity. Canadians – in their dozy way – have to face the odd bit of snow, though generally none of the meteorological and geological calamities of their cousins to the south. But the Canadians are a reminder that merely living in North America is not enough to create the spirit of the United States. The roughness of the neighbourhood is – as the philosophers put it – a necessary cause of Americanness, but it is not sufficient.

Chapter Five

THERE ARE VERY few occasions on which I want to strangle American friends, but the temptation becomes almost insurmountable when I hear them say: "Oh my Gosh!"

What they mean is: "Oh my God!"

But in polite American society, even this mild blasphemy is unacceptable.

So people hedge their bets, mind their language and blur the edges. The result is that life in the American suburbs is lived, linguistically at least, in soft focus "la-la land".

People warble rather than talk, and inoffensiveness is raised to the status of a major virtue. Don't get me wrong; American politeness is a major virtue – but American linguistic timidity is a vice. You see it especially at Christmas, which has now become "the holidays" in all but the deepest reaches of the Bible belt. Why? Out of fear of offending atheists, or Jews, or occultists, or Moslems or Hindus? It is potty. For one thing, none of the above-mentioned could possibly be offended, or if they were, they should not be; wishing someone a happy Christmas cannot be considered an act of aggression, cultural or otherwise. But more importantly, isn't your nation all about assimilation? Isn't it all about adherence to the core values of the Anglo-Protestant settlers who landed at Plymouth Rock and kicked the whole game off? Americans might not put it as starkly as that but in a nation in which ninety-something per cent believe in God, it does seem odd to me that the word Christmas is so underused. I long to hear someone say: "For God's sake, have a happy Christmas…"

If you think too much about the offence you might cause by telling someone something, you begin to lose track of what the something might be. You begin to value everyone being happy above anyone knowing the truth. An example: the *New York Times*, self-styled newspaper of record, printed an obituary for Earl Butz, a little-remembered politician from the Nixon era who had finally come unstuck campaigning for Nixon's successor:

> Mr. Ford had been counting on Mr. Butz to help win the Midwestern farm vote when he ran for a full

term against Jimmy Carter in 1976, and Mr. Butz campaigned strenuously in that race. But his career in Washington suddenly ended a month before the election. On a plane trip following the Republican National Convention in August, accompanied by, among others, John W. Dean 3rd, the former White House counsel, Mr. Butz made a remark in which he described blacks as "coloreds" who wanted only three things – satisfying sex, loose shoes and a warm bathroom – desires that Mr. Butz listed in obscene and scatological terms.

I read that piece and wondered at its coyness. The late journalist and author Christopher Hitchens, implacable enemy of the inoffensive, was on hand to let rip:

There isn't a grown-up person with a memory of 1976 who doesn't recall that Butz said that Americans of African descent required only "a tight pussy, loose shoes, and a warm place to shit." Had this witless bigotry not been reported accurately, he might have held onto his job. But any reader of the paper who was less than 50 years old could have read right past the relevant sentence without having the least idea of what the original controversy had been about. What on earth is the point of a newspaper of record that decides that the record itself may be too much for us to bear?

Hitchens went on to make a wider and more political point about the failure of American newspapers to re-print the images of Mohammed commissioned by that Danish newspaper in 2005. The cartoons were, of course, printed legally in a free society but in the months after they appeared there was, you will remember, an effort to intimidate the Western media into silence and apologies and quiescence. Americans – for all the freedom talk – were pretty near the back when it came to standing up for the Danes. Inoffensiveness morphs into cowardice, in other words. Failure to speak clearly, even if offence might be caused, becomes a failure to confront issues at all, a failure in the case of the Danish cartoons to stand up for freedom against tyranny. I suspect Hitchens might be wrong about the Danish cartoons or at least guilty of simplifying a more complex issue (the problem seems to me exaggerated respect for religion, any religion, rather than over-dainty concern for causing offence), but the thrust of his case is true: the American mainstream media plays safe. Too safe.

It does so because it is largely commercially driven – who wants to offend viewers when the name of the game is gaining viewers? But there is a deeper, more interesting reason for this timidity. It is cultural. Perhaps as a reaction to the roughness of the place, to the harsh Wild West saloon bar that America partly is, a suburban culture has been developed that deodorises the tangy scent of controversy of everyday life. It is like keeping good cheese in the fridge. It minimises nasty smells at the expense of the richness of the experience of life. It makes you want to scream: "Enough fucking cleanliness!"

I have a friend from New Zealand who lives in the Washington DC suburbs – a normal chap and the father of three very nicely spoken children – who admitted to me that he craves indecent language so badly that he goes to the video store and takes out British films. *Sexy Beast*, set among British gangsters in the Costa del Crime, is his favourite, because some of the sentences are comprised only of swear-words. Most Americans in "la-la land" would find even the title of that film problematic. *Sexy Beast*! "Oh my gosh!" The word sex, used in the context of fun, or in a slightly racy manner, is not normally to be heard on your side of the Atlantic. And it is not just the word. The whole world of sexual behaviour is closed to American polite society.

Eroticism is anathema in the United States – in advertising, in art, in thought.

It is not the greatest of America's issues, I suppose, but to English eyes American exceptionalism in this area renders the place deeply strange. It tends to lead us to wonder about the fundamentals of American society and of the American way of life; it is, therefore, worthy of study.

What seems to be the problem? America is the centre of two sex industries, the pornography trade based in Los Angeles, and the abstinence trade, based in Middle America but with branch offices all over the nation. Both of these trades have global reach: US porn is of course omnipresent, but US views on abstinence and abortion have also had a global impact on the battle against AIDS. And they are connected at home too: to put it crudely, sex and sin are dangerously interlinked in the minds of too many Americans. America is one of the least erotic places on earth – on television there is a choice, basically, between mainstream pap in which sex is smut, to be giggled at or airbrushed away, and hard-core drivel in which serial couplings are portrayed in gynaecological detail stripped of humanity and appeal. (Folks, I am imagining this from the titles.)

There is nothing in between. A recent American radio report about a museum of erotica that had just opened in Oxford, England, brought it home. No one had complained! The American reporter simply couldn't believe it – and was so conditioned to the words sex and complaint going together that she could not cope. She did her best to describe the museum and interview the curator but the lack of complaints was for her the biggest deal by far.

The fact is that any American reporter covering any subject with any tangential link to sex risks his or her job.

Imagine then, the upset and the outrage, the gaping open-mouthed horror, when on the programme with the biggest audience of the year – the annual Super Bowl football match – the Janet Jackson incident occurred. You may remember it, but if you are British I doubt the memory is one of your most searing. In the United States, it lives on. To recap the nightmare – look away if you must – 90 million people watching the half-time show saw her frock fall apart and reveal one of her breasts.

For many of the viewers it seems the experience was one of the most shocking of their lives. "Oh my gosh," they collectively intoned. Within days, you will remember, there were hearings on Capitol Hill (I am not making this up) and earnest discussions on talk shows about how to save America from indecency. I saw a breakfast television presenter tell a solemn-looking weather person that her nine-year-old son had been watching. Imagine. What will she tell him? What will he think? Well, I hope he has a good memory, that young chap, because the powers that be have been coming down hard ever since on breasts and on talk of breasts.

Within days of the Janet Jackson incident, a partial view of an elderly woman's top half on a medical drama programme was hastily cut. The programme was made by the BBC and shown in full on BBC1. In America, it could not now be broadcast. The subject matter – a dirty bomb – can be discussed. They have a copy of this film in the Homeland Security office that deals with domestic nuclear threats (I know: they showed it to me) but realistic portrayal of the reaction, doctors coping with the aftermath, could not and cannot even now be shown to the wider

American public. And it wasn't the bomb, stupid, it was the breast.

Of course, as relaxed Europeans would tell you if only you would listen, the effort to desexualise all of public life results not only in very dull television, but in an underbelly of seediness – which is the only place left for it to go. It leads to Victorian England: chintzy gentility and child prostitution living side by side.

It also leads, in modern America, to disaster, personal and familial. I have lost count of the times, in the many years I lived among you, that an upstanding pillar of the community has been laid low by a sex scandal. And they almost never involve what one might call traditional sex between chaps and girls. In fact, quite often they don't really involve sex at all, but the whiff of it is enough. The whiff of sex and the stench of hypocrisy as human beings try to live their lives according to the bizarre and unnatural precepts of America's permanent war on eroticism.

Before 2006, most Americans would never have heard of Mark Foley. He was a minor congressman from Florida; once thought of as a potential recruit to the Senate but quickly passed over. Nobody outside Florida or Capitol Hill had ever heard of him. Then Mr Foley, a Republican, was forced to resign after sending salacious messages to teenage male pages in the House of Representatives. The pages are essentially interns, sent by their proud parents to run messages around the corridors of Congress. Mr Foley had texted some of them his naughtiest thoughts. Ghastly indeed, and several complained. Two points struck me, though. First, in spite of an FBI investigation, no charges were ever brought against Mr Foley. He broke no law. Secondly, hadn't his really odious behaviour come years earlier when he introduced a bill, the "Child Modelling Exploitation Prevention Act of 2002" to outlaw websites featuring images of children, saying that "these websites are nothing more than a fix for paedophiles". Legal experts complained that the bill would have prohibited commercial photography of children, in other words, the United States would have become the first nation on earth to ban pictures of kids out of fear that its citizens were sent into a sexual frenzy by them.

Was Mr Foley a weirdo? You bet, but paging the pages was the least of his sins.

Another case in point was the very strange business of Ted Haggard and the male prostitute. Pastor Haggard, you will remember, was one of those squeaky-clean-looking evangelical TV people, the ones who are (to cynical English eyes) so obviously not what they seem, that only in a nation as closed to sex as America is could they survive. Anyway, the pastor used to rail against gay marriage, citing it as a threat to the entire institution of marriage, apple pie etc. Then, of course, he was found to have been having a three-year-long tryst with a gay prostitute with whom he took methamphetamine, a serious drug. Now plainly, Mr Haggard was troubled, but would he have had these personal issues if his ministry, his entire public life, had not been spent so closely focused on sex? Like the Roman Catholic Church at its worst, America has an unhealthy obsession with sexual behaviour, and an inability to find a niche for it in the life of the nation that allows it to become, well, normal.

This brings us to America's continuing problem with the rational world. I don't buy the whole package of disdain that tends to accompany European attitudes to American religion. America's rational world problem is caused by something other than its Christian faith, and it thrives in areas of life that are not in the least bit religious. Halloween is the obvious example – the Celtic festival came to the US with Irish immigrants but took off in the New World with a vigour that suggests a deep-seated desire to wallow in ghosts and goblins and fear of dark forces. My children love it, of course, but every Halloween, as we traipsed around the neighbourhood picking up sweets and admiring pumpkin heads, I felt an uneasy sense that this festival should not be quite the big deal that it is; something is amiss.

Many evangelical Christians agree. But who are they to talk? God in his heaven must sometimes wonder at the sheer credulousness of some of his more ardent US followers. It is, truth be told, a credulousness that renders large numbers of Americans unfit to play a major role in the intellectual life of the 21st century; unfit for any role with a speaking part and certainly unfit for leadership. American religious faith was described to me once as infantile; that is too offensive a term to be useful, I think, but the charge is interesting. I suppose I should accept my own logic and try to understand that the American religious revivals – they are episodic events – come, at least in part, as a result of the search for a better, happier world on which to focus. And it is a fact that the toughest of environments, natural and man-made, have tended to breed the most religious of souls.

We talk about the US being a religious place, and it is, but the South is where the spooky action is. The South is where church attendance really is above 50 per cent – close to 60 per cent in states like Alabama and Louisiana. Drive around the South on a Sunday morning and the chapel car parks are filled to overflowing with *Dukes of Hazard* pick-up trucks. There's a mini rush hour when the faithful all drive home, spitting chewing tobacco out of their broken side windows into the ditches bordering the endless space of the fields.

My problem, though, is not that all these folks go to church; it is what they are told while they are there and the way in which it translates into a crass and superstitious view of all human life. It is the effect of tin pot theology on their capacity to think straight, and by extension on America's capacity to make decent judgements – in science, of course, but in ethics as well.

An example that depressed me: a Tuesday afternoon outside the statehouse in Atlanta, Georgia.

You know and I know at least a short list of things about Atlanta. It is a modern city. It has one of the busiest airports in the world. It is home to CNN. It is where Martin Luther King preached. It has a literary pedigree as well: *Gone with the Wind* was written there. And yet on this Tuesday afternoon, the top brass of the state – led by the Governor himself (the admirably named Sonny Perdue) – had gathered not to honour human achievement or plan human improvement, but to pray for rain.

That's right. They stood on the steps of the state-house, 250 of them, and closed their eyes and looked to the heavens. "We have not been good stewards of our land," they murmured. "We have not been good stewards of our water. Lord, have mercy on your people, have mercy on us and grant us rain. Oh God, let rain fall on this land of Georgia."

Stone Age men possessed of undeveloped brains and little knowledge of the natural world would have recognised the gathering and felt quite at home. So would many anti-modernist Moslem extremists, the characters who live in caves in Afghanistan and dream of chopping off our heads. Godforsaken simple people from throughout the sad superstitious history of humanity could have had a ball on that Atlanta

Tuesday. I felt sad for a nation not fully in control of its senses. Sad as well for people so truly incapable of empathy for others who really were in dire need of God's assistance but who were not receiving it. Sad that this pathetic gathering could be so self-satisfied, so cruelly uncaring about the suffering elsewhere in the world, that they really thought God would drop his other concerns and listen to their prating on about rain. Sad that rich people in the richest nation on the face of the earth have not got the gumption to feel any of the humility that (they told me at my Quaker school) the Bible teaches.

That is the problem with the simple theologies of the South; they are destructive of educated thought and destructive of a true sense of common humanity. It is not just nonsense, it is dangerous nonsense.

Now you want to know if it did rain. It did! They chose a day with a twenty-per-cent chance and on CNN they had a weatherman report it as a kind of miracle. Shame on them.

There is a postscript to this silly little incident, though, and it is important because again it demonstrates that "the picture" in this complex and freedom-loving nation is never "the whole picture".

I noticed a few days later that the blogspace in the *Atlanta Journal* newspaper was filled with comments, overwhelmingly hostile to the batty Governor and his Stone Age cohorts. Typical was this from a writer who identified himself as broker627:

> SCARY!! Our government leaders are asking invisible spirits that are floating around for help with our water issue. REMINDER – HE HAS BEEN "PRAYING" FOR RAIN SINCE WE MOVED HERE IN APRIL WITH NO RESULTS SO IT'S ALL B.S.!!!" I don't believe in any of it but if I did, we should be praying for a new governor.

My favourite, though, was this pithy cry, so pellucid and so true, from LD in Atlanta: "Good Grief, how embarrassing."

It *is* embarrassing. But I come back to the point that this is not really about religion per se but about a kind of chronic mental failure that seems to haunt the nation. Opinion polls suggest, for instance, that roughly a fifth of all Americans – really one in five – believe that the sun goes around the earth. This is more than ignorance. This is Stone Age stuff. And if you can believe that, you can – really – believe anything. During the height of the controversy over

Barack Obama's egocentric and bombastic former pastor, the Rev. Jeremiah Wright, one of the central issues was Wright's view that HIV might have been created by the US government to get rid of ethnic minorities. It was that belief, and Wright's refusal to back down from it, that led directly to Obama's final decision to cut the preacher adrift in April 2008. But as the *New York Times* journalist Nicholas Kristof pointed out, opinion polls suggested as many as 30 per cent of black Americans thought that the charge was at least plausible. When Kristof was deluged with messages from white Americans expressing incredulity at this figure, he responded by pointing out that white America was also no stranger to conspiracy theory madness; for instance, according to a poll conducted by Ohio University, 36 per cent of all Americans asked thought US government officials might have allowed 9/11 to happen in order to bring about war in the Middle East. Kristof ended this thought with a depressing flourish: "Americans are as likely to believe in flying saucers as in evolution. Depending on how the questions are asked, roughly 30 to 40 per cent of Americans believe in each."

Incidentally, Mr Kristof is a campaigner for better education – more math, more science – in the belief, apparently, that this might do the trick. He thinks the nation has dumbed itself down but might be capable, with some effort, of climbing out of the pit of ignorance. I have my doubts. There is something visceral about American credulousness. Something Europeans, quite rightly, find inexplicable and frightening; and just plain wrong.

Chapter Six

ONE OF THE first acts of the Obama administration –
before they tackled the economic crisis and began the
long struggle that would change the health system,
well before they began the effort to come to grips
with Afghanistan, or engaged with Russia, or tried
and failed to close Guantanamo, or shot Osama bin
Laden – was the removal of a bust of Sir Winston
Churchill from the Oval Office.

It was reported at the time that they chucked
poor Winston in a taxi and sent him home to the
British embassy. It appeared to be an act of gross
callousness, particularly given the fact that most
Washington taxis are driven by cheerful Ethiopians
with little knowledge of the streets outside central
Addis Ababa. Winston might have ended up in
some flop-house in crime-ridden Southeast DC,
a doorstop for a drug dealer's moll, or worse. The
news was broken by the ever-energetic and well-

connected Tom Baldwin, then of the *Times*, a trad-itionalist with a sense of history first encouraged, no doubt, by his tutors at Balliol College, Oxford. But Tom's story was followed up by less well-educated and more excitable British newspaper reporters who reached for predictable tropes when they found out: *Britain snubbed by the new President! The special rela-tionship itself sent packing in a cab!* There was even a motive found: Churchill's crackdown on the Mau Mau rebels in Kenya had led to the imprisonment of Obama's paternal grandfather. *It was revenge!* In spite of the fact that Obama's relationship with his father was (famously) distant and with his grand-father genuinely non-existent, nothing got in the way of the narrative that this was a snub delivered to an old ally.

Months later I was in the White House talking to a senior official. "Why did you do it?" I asked.

"You folks are obsessed," was his reply. "We were just clearing house. We didn't even know who it was... We thought it was Eisenhower: elderly white folks all look alike to us."

He was only half joking.

It is not that the Obama administration had any particular dislike for Britain and the British. Exacting revenge for the wrongs done to the Mau Mau was way down their to-do list, frankly somewhere near the bottom. It had never been mentioned on the campaign trail (how delicious if it had been: "Ohio, I make this pledge to you, we are Americans and as Americans we know that the Mau Mau's values are our values"). But what the British press picked up, what they sensed right from the start, what caused them to be prickly and dyspeptic, was that the focus of this President was not on us and never would be. Americans thought we might have noticed this by now. To sophisticated East Coast commentators, the demise of Britain – *lost an empire and not yet found a role* – is nothing new to report; a *Newsweek* article about the Churchill flap raised its journalistic eyebrow and enquired, laconically: "Has America's even-tempered new President already ruffled feathers in the land that spawned Borat and Benny Hill?"

And Churchill! our papers screamed. *We spawned him as well! Quite recently!* But most of America was having none of it, and in those heady days before the Obama presidency fell from grace, most Americans backed him, if they even noticed the row at all.

So just to make the point, we had another. Prime Minister Gordon Brown came to Washington and to

the White House and was treated with what the hyper-
ventilating British press (even those who regarded
Brown as a villain) saw as grotesque discourtesy.
Amid a list of complaints that was, as one American
paper sniffed, "longer than Magna Carta", was that
the Browns gave the President a rather fancy gift and
received utter tat in return. The facts suggest… well,
that it was true. The Brown gift was a pen-holder
crafted from the timbers of the nineteenth-century
British anti-slaving warship HMS *President* (whose
sister ship, HMS *Resolute*, provided the wood for the
Oval Office's desk). Not bad. Thoughtful. Tasteful.
Au point. The Obama gift was – as you doubtless
remember because it was the moment you began
to think that Obama was less than a full saint – 25
DVDs of American movies. *He's Just Not That Into
You* was not one of them, but reading between the
lines that was the message. Less reported at the time
but equally careless: the gifts for the Brown children
were models of Marine One, the presidential heli-
copter. You can get these anywhere, including the
White House gift shop, which is where they probably came from. The whole visit was a mess, a *train
wreck*, to use the wonderful American expression.
Didn't Obama care? Didn't he *know* about *us?* Hadn't

someone warned the new President that everything hinged on America's relationship with the Brits?

Evidently not. And here is why not: because it does not. Whether it is special or whether it is essential, it is, like the Monty Python parrot, an ex-relationship. Fine words in Westminster Hall do not change that fact.

The lofty view first: when you place the so-called special relationship alongside the relationship the US has with China, with Russia, with the EU, with Israel and the Palestinians, with Iran, with Iraq, with Pakistan, with India, with emerging nations such as Brazil – well, you hear what I am saying: it ain't that special.

David Cameron made much of seeking new partnerships in his foreign policy, and the same goes for the Americans. More than any other recent presidency, the Obama administration needs to make the case to the American people that the world's only superpower must recalibrate its relationship with the rest of the planet. This is partly the result of setbacks America experienced following the hubris and the indebtedness of the Bush years, but partly too it is the result of the rise of the rest of the world, the emergence of China and India and Brazil, the stubborn refusal of Russia to fade into memory. Drinking Scotch with British prime ministers, while fiddling absent-mindedly with the head of Winston Churchill and listening to a tape of Edward Murrow, does not really do it. The Obama administration was rather rude to Gordon Brown. The gifts were not desperately well thought through, but the debacle illustrated an important point. The special relationship does not exist. This President, and any modern American president, must be interested primarily in reaching out to other nations. Henry Kissinger is said to have wanted a number to call when he wanted to speak to Europe: now we have a number (step forward Baroness Ashton, the EU Foreign Minister) but they ain't calling any more except as an occasionally remembered courtesy. Times have changed. I saw Henry Kissinger in London in 2011 and he spoke warmly about the special relationship, but quite what it was, he could not clearly say. It's like a ghost, or an imaginary friend in the airing cupboard. It's private: it is a creature of the mind rather than the real world.

Shortly after President Obama was elected, a frustrated viewer wrote to the BBC. Why, he demanded, had the corporation not thought to send Justin Webb to interview the new man? Was it not recognised that this would be interesting? Were we not aware that this presidency would be consequential and did we not think it worth expending a little energy, a taxi fare at least, in getting the scoop? Ah, if only he knew. We had, in truth, come up with the idea of interviewing Obama ourselves. Indeed, during the campaign I had tried repeatedly to persuade his senior staff that the presidential candidate might care to signal how different he was by granting a sit-down interview to a foreigner. "I hear what you say" was as far as it went. I thought at one stage that I might change their minds by catching a ground-breaking few minutes with the great rival for the Democratic Party nomination, Hillary Clinton. I managed to get face to face with her on a rope-line in New Hampshire and launched into my exclusive chat. She smiled at the man in front of me and the child beside me. She answered a question posed by an elderly woman to my left about her brooch. Then she moved on, unmoved by my second question or my third or fourth or fifth. She blanked me more comprehensively than I have ever been blanked by anyone before. Special relationship?

What I am saying is that it was quite a big deal when we finally made it to the library of the White House and to those two chairs facing each other. To celebrate (as we waited for him), I moved them closer together, perhaps in subliminal homage to the special relationship that might see our toes touch where the Japanese reporter or the Swiss would be kept at a distance. But alas, the rules were the same. A flunky leapt forward: "Sir, step away from the chairs!" Apparently, they are placed by protocol officials and no one, not even Winston Churchill himself, is allowed to move them. Even Andrew Marr, who followed me to the White House in 2011, was not, I was pleased to see, allowed too close.

The entire experience of interviewing Obama served to underline the death of the special relationship. The White House, to their credit, never came close to vetting what questions I was going to ask, but they made it clear that their central concern was whether the interview would be translated and replayed by the World Service. They had no interest in impressing the folks in Chipping Sodbury. Let them (try to) watch DVDs. Obama wanted to use the BBC to speak to the world. The approach was repeated a year later when the White House granted the BBC its second interview with the President. It could have gone to my successor in Washington or to Andrew Marr or John Humphrys or Adrian Chiles and Christine Bleakley, who were still on the *One Show* sofa and still on the up. It did not. It went to Bakman Kalbassi of the BBC Persian Service. And my information is that the White House was delighted with the results, a strong interview in which the President was pressed hard to give firm answers, and those answers were delivered directly, via a trustworthy translation, into homes in Iran.

So the fact that the President eventually sat down with Andrew Marr, just before coming to Britain on the "essential relationship" tour, should be seen in the context of initial concern with the outside world. Andy's interview will have been used on BBC World and that is where the White House will have wanted it to be used.

Sometimes the British people, and British institutions such as the BBC or the Army, can be of use to American administrations. Often you admire the Brits (certainly true in the case of the Army and to a lesser extent the BBC), but it is never about Britain or about the relationship with Britain. There is always more to it. It is about what Britain can do.

It is, to quote the man who received the DVDs, "a partnership of purpose". We offer the partnership, he might have added, and they offer the purpose.

When the House of Commons Select Committee on Foreign Affairs declared the special relationship over in their report of 2009, the committee chairman, Mike Gapes, officiated at the funeral. I had given evidence to the committee, so I had an inkling of where they were going, but the words used by Mr Gapes are still worth noting:

> The use of the phrase "the special relationship" in its historical sense, to describe the totality of the ever-evolving UK–US relationship, is potentially misleading, and we recommend that its use should be avoided.
>
> Yes, we have a special relationship with the US, but we must remember that so too do other countries including regional neighbours, strategic allies and partners. British and European politicians have been guilty of over-optimism about the extent of influence they have over the US. We must be realistic and accept that globalisation, structural changes and shifts in geopolitical power will inevitably affect the UK–US relationship.
>
> RIP.

And yet. There is a place where the special relationship – not essential but special – still exists. I have been there. Mr Gapes and his committee, by visiting Washington and Washington alone, have not. There are no direct flights from Britain. You have to change. You have to fly on into that pancake bit in the middle of America where, on a cloudless day, the view stretches towards the horizon. Flat farmland and grids of roads with, it seems from 30,000 feet, no cars. If the Foreign Affairs Committee had managed to slip away from the embassy dinner and the congressional visit and gone down to Reagan Airport (Washington's domestic hub), they could have boarded a flight to somewhere in Middle America – Boise, Idaho, or Wichita, Kansas, or Normal, Illinois (I think you have to change again for Normal but heck, this isn't a timetable), and there the picture would have been very different. There, to be British (alright, English) really counts.

This is the part of America where Tony Blair's journey never ends. Prime Minister Blair (always *Prime Minister*) and Lady Thatcher have morphed into a composite picture of the plucky dependable Brit. Both are revered, and through their good offices, gentle reader, any Englishman and woman who is not actually a mass murderer, can be too. But to assume that the attraction is our British muscularity (or Blair's and Thatcher's), or our ability to commit English troops to faraway wars, or our (imagined or otherwise) support or past support for these political giants and their policies, is to make a serious mistake.

You love us for our vowels. Imagine an Englishman arriving in Boise or Wichita or Normal. He is in need of refreshment and spots, in the out-of-town mall between the airport and the hotel, a Starbucks. In he goes and orders a muffin and an iced tea. Pandemoniun ensues. Folks are called in from the back office: "Jolene, come here and listen to this man's beautiful voice!" Large ladies with serious religious views consider throwing away their chances of getting to heaven for a moment of madness with this English stranger. You can see it in their eyes. he is glamour. Like Julia Roberts popping into that bookshop in Notting Hill, he causes hearts to flutter.

"Oh, my gosh!" they murmur, as he places his order for a second time, for the cameras, as it were.

I know this because I have done it. I spent much of my eight years working for the BBC in America shamelessly hamming up my Englishness.

If impersonating Hugh Grant in a public place is a crime then I must plead guilty. It opens doors. So many Americans love it. Those who do feel they know us and they know that we know the Queen, so when they shake our hands they are shaking hers too. I know it didn't work for BP's Tony Hayward but poor Mr Hayward is the exception that proves the rule. And, to an extent, this Starbucks relationship matters. It puts us at an advantage, for instance, over the Germans. My former colleague Matt Frei (a well known figure in British TV news) is an English-educated polyglot of staggering ability, and could easily have revealed himself to be (as he is) German by birth and nationality. Did he? I don't think so. In Boise he was English. The full monty: Westminster and Oxford.

This, of course, is not the special relationship of which the politicians speak. They hardly notice it. It is not documented. It is certainly not essential. But it is real. It will make a difference to an Englishman who goes to Normal. It will not get him out of jail, or have him feted if he's accused of destroying an entire national coastline with his carelessly spilled oil. But it will give him the benefit of the doubt if he scrapes the sheriff's car while parking. It will reduce speeding tickets: "Officer, as an Englishman, I offer the profoundest of apologies." Sometimes it will afford him special protection. In Corning, Iowa just before the 2008 caucus, I had illegally parked our large crew car outside a café. It was very, very cold, so I volunteered to stay in the vehicle while a producer went in to get the drinks. Behind me a police cruiser pulled up and the officer got out and approached. Obviously he was going to move me on; I was, after all, committing a crime as serious as any he was likely to come across that day. But no: on hearing my accent, the gentle cop demanded that I go into the café as well and warm up and have a real good stay. He would look after the car. Which is what he did, with his lights flashing, until we were ready to move on. To deny the special relationship, in the light of this behaviour, seems churlish in the extreme. You Americans like us. You do. You sometimes find us a bit ungodly and a bit over-complicated (though fixed-term parliaments will help here) but you fundamentally believe that we are on the right side, provided we can keep our snobbiness at bay. This is an important point: if we hector Middle Americans as the *Guardian* famously did just before the 2004 election, encouraging readers to write personal letters to voters in Ohio imploring them not to vote for George W. Bush, our accents will begin to grate. The areas targeted by the *Guardian* swung suspiciously towards the sitting President and away from the course of action, a vote for the Democrat John Kerry, that the *Guardian* readers were advocating. I visited a town where some letters had dropped on doormats and the response was fascinating. They were so pleased to see me that the local paper came and took photos. I had to eat for England. But the letters with Islington postmarks had caused deep offence; the revolutionary war was rekindled in an instant.

But when we talk nicely, you listen. We have a window seat in the Starbucks of Middle America. We are – you think – comfortably familiar. We are not truly foreign. I sensed that at McCain/Palin rallies in 2008, where although quite a few folks associated the BBC with socialism (Rupert Murdoch's message penetrates the boondocks), most were very friendly. They are not so well disposed to all foreigners in these parts. At a town hall meeting I attended, a woman seized the microphone and praised Senator McCain to the rafters while he beamed and grinned. "Obama is not good for America," she asserted. "Yes, ma'am," McCain chirruped. "Obama is a socialist." "Yes, ma'am." "He's an Ay-rab!"

An Ay-rab? McCain looked panicked. This was barmy talk which he instantly knew would look bad outside this small town. He seized the microphone and delivered an unintentionally revealing rebuke: "Ma'am, Senator Obama is not an Ay-rab: he is a family man..."

Which said it all. We are family men, we Brits. Nobody in Middle America would question it and that gives us standing.

But there is a problem and you, as an American with an interest in the outside world's view of you (why else would you have read this far?), will already have spotted it. These Americans who regard us as special, who find our accents mellifluous, are not necessarily in the driving seat in the modern United States. Middle Americans who have been making the running in recent times, Sarah Palin's Tea Party crowd, tend to find us less appealing because of our lack of religious spine and our attachment to train travel and carbon trading. The gentler folk, supporters neither of Palin nor Obama, are rather lost when it comes to political clout.

And outside Middle America, where the real business of the nation is done, where the future lives, in towns like San Antonio, Texas, or Phoenix, Arizona, in the Starbucks there the English accent, amigo, counts for little. The problem for the special relationship based on what you might call the *Mayflower* Memory Syndrome is that the *Mayflower* rememberers are not in the driving seat in their nation. Obama's America – black, Hispanic, mixed-race America, future America – does not give a button for Olde England. It is coming up to 400 years since the *Mayflower* sailed to the New World. Memories have dimmed. A teenager with a Croatian immigrant mother and a Vietnamese immigrant father, planning to marry a Mexican immigrant girlfriend next year, will have little sense of the United Kingdom.

Already you can see the dominance of non-Hispanic white people, who today account for two-thirds of Americans, shaping up for dramatic collapse. Two-thirds today – but the census folks say they will be half the population in 2042 and 46 per cent by 2050. In the opposite trajectory, those who describe themselves as Hispanic, black, Asian and Native American will increase in proportion from about a third now to 54 per cent by 2050. Hispanics alone will make up 30 per cent of the nation. This is a new revolution – one of the most far-reaching changes in a country's racial and ethnic make-up in history, every bit as dramatic as the huge influx of Italian, Irish and Eastern European immigrants that transformed the US in the early twentieth century.

The shift in majority status from non-Hispanic whites, who have enjoyed the dominant position since the gang who sailed in the *Mayflower* arrived in New England and survived that first winter, is going to have profound implications. In the long term, it may well lead to a sea-change in your country's understanding of its politics and culture, but already, I would argue, it is leading to a new sense of its relationships with the outside world. For this reminted version of America is going to look from the much broader perspective of its heritage on the various outside powers competing for attention.

To put it bluntly: the Hugh Grant stuff cuts no ice with these brown folk. And this – fundamentally – is why the Commons Foreign Affairs Committee was right and the sentimentalists of the British press are wrong. Change has come. Though the extent of future change, the kind of change that sees Matt Frei as happy to be German as English in Boise, is an open question and an interesting one. It is here that the echoes of the special relationship may or may not count for something in the coming decades. For America has a choice to make. It is not a choice between being cosy with the English or not cosy with the English. It is a much more interesting and profound choice about the kind of nation that you in the US want to have, and the choice impacts directly on us.

America is mad as hell. The recession – which the *Sunday Times* economics editor Anatole Kaletsky eye-catchingly suggests could have a longer-term and deeper impact on America than 9/11 – has knocked for six some of the central pieces of American political furniture. I accept that; other books will focus on what happened and why. My interest is in one area: America's sense of itself and of what it means to be American. Shortly after he became President, a friend of mine asked Barack Obama whether he believed in American exceptionalism. "Hot Damn," he replied, "the USA rules and always will." No, of course he didn't say that. In fact, he didn't say anything much, except that he was sure Greeks believed in Greek exceptionalism and he regarded America in the same way. This is a cop-out. The general view across the political divide in the US is that the nation, if not divinely invested with the purpose of improving humanity, is or should be mighty well qualified to do the job. The right stresses strength and the left stresses example but both sides in American politics are pretty sure that America is qualitatively different from the rest of the industrialised world. And at the heart of the enterprise is the American Creed. Now that creed – hard work, old-style religion etc – the pioneer creed upon which America is based, comes from the *Mayflower*.

There is a lively historical controversy about the motives of the original *Mayflower* passengers. Part of the reason they made the ghastly journey west was religious persecution, but partly as well it was an economic decision – they thought they could make a totally new life. But the central, most important point is that these people were not (as the failed Virginia settlers had been) aristocrats out to make a buck. They were the dispossessed. That is America's seed-corn: to have nothing and gamble everything. The boat arrived in Plymouth, Massachusetts, and the character of America was forged in the horror of the early efforts to stay alive, the mistreatment by and mistreatment of the Native Americans, and the long tear-strewn and hope-strewn march west. If America is an idea as much as a place, then the idea was born in the *Mayflower* and honed by the future generations who would throw the British out and forge the strongest country on earth. There are around 600 American families who trace their ancestry to the *Mayflower*. They are the slim but sinewy trunk of the multi-branched tree.

Or are they? This is what you Americans have to decide. The exceptionalist places the creed and the attachment to a set of values, a narrative, at the heart of the nation. The waves of immigrants who arrived in New York harbour in the nineteenth and twentieth centuries were almost all of them arriving blind, in the sense that they could have no conception of what the future held for them. They were, generally, banned from having any kind of employment already arranged. They were to be social virgins. It was not quite *Mayflower* conditions but their lives were, in many cases, pretty awful. For modern-day immigrants, from Benin or South Korea or Mexico, life is much easier. A pre-arranged job is often required rather than banned. But the idea is still that when you arrive in America you sign up for something, and something more than just the basic citizenship ceremony. You sign up for the *Mayflower*. For individualism tempered by community support, for Puritanism tempered by a belief in happiness. You leave your baggage at home or, if you bring it, you leave it largely unpacked. This, of course, is the opposite of multiculturalism. It does not celebrate the traditions and the whacky beliefs of your fore-fathers. It does not even begin to toy with the idea that you should live in your own community and speak your mother tongue and never mix with the rest of the nation. That would be un-American.

But here is the issue. If America becomes steadily more heterogeneous – and that is a given – does it also lose sight of the history of how it came to be great? In particular, does it lose sight of the links with Europe and that creed that has been handed down from generation to generation? To put it crudely: when white America dies, will the *Mayflower* go down with it? And white America will die, in the sense of being the dominant force in the nation, and it will do so quite soon; of that there seems to be no real doubt. Change, you could argue, has actu-ally not yet come – but it is around the corner. It is an interesting fact that the demographic revolution I have referred to in this chapter is also going to have a generational impact. White folks will be old. Already, nearly half of all American children under five come from minority communities. By the middle of the century, more than 60 per cent of American children will not be white. This matters in all kinds of ways, and, being Americans, most of you will see it as an opportunity to be seized. Nonetheless, this seizing of the future might involve a break with the past – and the ghosts of the past – that the nation has never before contemplated. America is already a tad hazy about its former greatest ally. A survey a few years ago found that many Americans thought the United Kingdom was somewhere off the Persian Gulf. But the real change comes when the nation has made a complete ethnic break with its past. That is when the old Protestant work ethic, the old sense of individualism, the old attachment to inequality and harshness that went alongside that individualism, might all begin to fall away. Where does it leave the special or essential relationship? Where does it leave Winston Churchill? Winston who?

On the other hand, perhaps a little distance might be beneficial. Shorn of the constant disappointment of the relationship, finally freed from the expectation that the President is going to call and ask our permission to sneeze or invade somewhere, perhaps this is the moment that we can relax and begin to get on better. Perhaps, too, we can escape from the self-disgust, the self-loathing even, that is brought on by the strain of trying to maintain to ourselves that our relationship is equal when we know in our hearts that it is not. And that escape could be consequential, allowing an insouciance to develop about some American traits and habits, particularly domestic oddities like execution or religiosity, that at the moment get us so steamed up because we are not influencing these matters in the way that you Yanks seem so effortlessly to invade and influence our own popular culture, even our language.

The former controller of BBC Radio Four, Mark Damazer, sent me a note years ago complaining about my use on air of the American phrase "going forward", a phrase you hear regularly now, especially among business people in England. My colleague John Humphrys carries on the battle – if he asks you how you are, do not, on pain of death, reply "good" – and the battle might or might not be one worth having (I will address it in detail in a later chapter); my point is that we would be more relaxed about our relationship with you, more cheerfully unruffled, if we did not have in the back of our minds the vague, unformed but powerful notion that we have to protect ourselves against a partner bent on abusing partnership and getting the better of us at every turn.

Chapter Seven

Americans are optimistic, friendly, inquisitive, practical-
minded. They find it difficult to believe that progress
is not inevitable. They do not easily accept the right to
reserve and privacy; they assume that if two men meet the
natural thing is for them to exchange experiences. They
have a distrust of theory. What interests them is the ability
to apply an idea to the solution of a problem; and they
reserve their supreme respect for men of the type of Ford
rather than men of the type of Theodore Richards.
Harold Laski, *The American Democracy*, 1949

THEODORE WHO? HE appears – googled – to be the
first American to win the Nobel Prize for Chemistry.
He suffered from depression and had two sons, both
of whom killed themselves. So Harold Laski has a
point here. Most Americans would indeed, socially
and psychologically, tend to sympathise more with

Ford. This wonderfully fusty piece of prose, penned by the doyen of English left-wing academics just after the war, brings home the full extent of the cultural separateness of Johnnie American (described here as you might describe a spaniel), but also the constancy of our view of you and its essential truth. Laski's description, up to and including Ford and poor old Theodore Wotsit, is as valid today as it was then. Laski is best known in Britain as a commentator on and critic of the great Labour government of 1945 – he was himself a chairman of the Labour Party and a dominant voice of the left, cited as a big influence by, among others, Ralph Miliband, the communist dad of the current leader of the British Labour Party. But this view of America and Americans came before the left turned against America. Much of what they admired – modernity and efficiency and the ability of every man to achieve his potential – was there to be seen in America and should still be there today if only Americans let it happen. Americans, said Laski, did not suffer from the human contradiction "of being either a nobleman without the means to live the noble life, or being a merchant or a peasant, and finding, even if he was successful, that these circles of social life to which he might aspire were beyond his hope of entry". They are, in other words, free of class. That characterisation, with a little tinkering, still holds true.

But Laski's American is also (and I wonder whether he noticed this when he came back from Yale to teach at the LSE in the 1920s) rather free of, well, fun. There has been a suspicion of the unconventional in American life since the founding of the republic and this suspicion, it seems to me, is what lies at the heart of America's problem with humour. Laski suggests – rightly maybe – that the stress on teamwork in order for the various goals of American life to be met when the nation was being set up is the heart of the problem. You can be a rugged individualist in certain areas but when it comes to cultural togetherness you have to toe the line. This is not a problem we Brits have.

So although Americans can be funny, although you can be quick-witted and sympathetic and worldly and wise, you cannot, in the field of humour, be British. I spoke at a small lunch shortly after coming back to London and, as I was leaving, a friend of mine who'd come along caught up with me and said: "You were rubbish. Truly awful. You've obviously never done it before. You need to practise." It was a sweet thing to say. As anyone British will immediately recognise, he was being highly complimentary in that good old British manner. (At least that's what I understood – Oh God, was I wrong? Please call me, friend, and confirm.)

I liked what he said, anyway. And it reminded me that the earnestness of American life was something I could never really celebrate. Americans who think you have done well will say: "You did great!" They will smile too, in case the message is unclear. There will be no deadpan and no room for misunderstanding. If you do badly they will walk away, embarrassed. In Britain, it's as if we are all sharing a long and not always particularly funny joke – a shaggy dog story whose end is not yet in sight but whose perambulations make us titter and feel that we know each other, and we like it that way. In our interactions in the drizzle – mordantly humorous, bleakly ironic – we celebrate life in our own twisted way.

Sometimes too twisted.

Crossing the road in south London shortly after arriving back, dazed from an early start at my new place of work, I slightly misjudged the distance between me and an oncoming car. This mistake could have inconvenienced the driver but only marginally. He might have had to take his foot off the accelerator but would have missed me easily if he had continued at his previous speed.

But he didn't. He speeded up! He still missed, I am delighted to say, because even at my advanced age I can still sidestep when necessary, but his intention was clear. He wanted to kill or maim the person crossing the road in front of him – or at least terrify the living daylights out of him.

This is not an isolated incident. You can see it on any street in any town in Britain. Drivers (and cyclists) speed up to make a point.

In America, in my experience, you do not do this. Barring Las Vegas – where a large proportion of drivers are desperate folks on their way home to explain to their wives that the last dollar has gone and they can't afford toilet paper any more – there is nowhere in the US where you would expect this to happen. American drivers slow down for pedestrians. You drive gently, respectfully. You do not employ irony behind the wheel.

At the end of the street where we lived in Washington, there was a four-way stop. It fascinated me. It worked. In fact, the only slight nuisance at these halts is the extreme politeness – *no, no, after you* – that can cause four cars simply to stop and wait for each other. No matter. I have come to miss the gentility of the four-way stop. It would not work in south London where I live now. Nor in Brussels, where I lived years ago and where the rules of the road are designed to make life as difficult and dangerous as possible for passengers and the less aggressive drivers. In Brussels they have a thing called *priorité à droite*. Folks arriving in a lane of traffic from the left have the right of way. They emerge without warning into the path of oncoming traffic. It makes for accidents and jerky, nervy driving. It is one of the reasons why Belgians hate each other with such unalloyed passion. The civilised Europeans, masters of the post-modern ironic universe, keepers of the flame of ancient learning, bash headlong into each other's cars with murderous rancour at any opportunity. You Americans hold back.

American gentility is a paradox, to put it mildly. There are aspects of American life that are bracing to the point of brutality: your health system, even post-Obama; your income disparities; your adherence (at least in the South) to a Christian faith that owes as much to the Old Testament as to the New; the mad, gaudy shoutiness of your politics in the modern age. But along with the harshness at the level of public life, there is a civility in normal suburban relations that Britain simply cannot match. Pervading every American equivalent of a British market town there is a calm and a harmony that puts one in mind of, well, Britain in the 1950s.

How do you do it? Guns and religion play a part. There is a yearning in the American psyche for well-disciplined order. Having no sense of irony leaves room for an overdeveloped sense of right and wrong. Relativism in the US is a love of relatives. But I reckon the greatest cause of America's calm is its patriotism. And not the type we normally notice. The American patriotism we all know too well – the flag and the flummery surrounding it – is only the tip of the nation-loving iceberg. The lower levels – the really solid levels on which the whole is built – are in communities in which they really do believe that "we are all in this together".

Truly believing that phrase makes a real difference. It causes people not just to pick up litter but not to drop it in the first place. It enables neighbourhoods to watch out for crime without any formal watch system being in place. It encourages volunteer fire services (our local service in Washington was wholly staffed by volunteers), and above all it prevents drivers from speeding up to hit pedestrians because... Well, why would you?

I freely admit that when we first came back to London, we wondered how people survived the city. The question never arose when I lived here as a student in the 1980s and as a youngish adult at various times since then. But after a decade away, and a return with young children and a more, shall we say, mature outlook on life, the capital city of my homeland seemed oddly frightening. I felt like a Kansas rube arriving in Manhattan in the 1970s. Your first thought is: *Vibrant!*; your second: *Help!*

Of course, modern Manhattan is now as peaceful as Nether Wallop. With New York taking its place among the world's more tranquil large cities – no murders at all in some weeks – much of the madness seems to have crossed the Atlantic. Almost everywhere you go in London, you are surrounded by deranged, dangerous people. After finishing my *Today* programme shift, I normally go home on the bus. The 148 is probably more frequent and certainly more comfortable than it would have been ten years ago but the people on the bus seem no happier. And when you step off it, you are in a land of almost comedic troubles. Walking home from the bus stop one morning, I paused to get money out of a cashpoint and found myself suddenly surrounded by sweaty, panting policemen. They were chasing someone, and they all piled into a café where the man might have been. A crowd gathered to watch the sport, several yelling encouragement, it wasn't clear to whom: the police or the man they were chasing. I pocketed my money and dashed. This scene would be unimaginable in the centres of most American cities. Outside the ghettos of the big cities, you will never, in America, see such street action.

And if you did, there would be a fuss. What strikes me on returning to Britain is how jaded we all are at the casual, low-level semi-violence that surrounds us. Interestingly, this is not new. The former Commissioner of the Metropolitan Police, Lord Blair, has written about the levels of violence that police officers come across in modern Britain. You would expect him to report that they are increasing. In fact, he says they are on the decrease. I find this perplexing because he should know. As should Sir Hugh Orde of the Association of Chief Police Officers, who privately took me to task once for suggesting that America seemed more peaceful than Britain. Perhaps the answer is that the kind of behaviour I find unsettling on returning to London is not really seen by today's police as violent. It is not even antisocial in any meaningful sense. But to me this behaviour is still odd and dysfunctional in a society where people ought really to be rubbing along.

An example: at Victoria Station in London the other day, a man – unremarkably dressed in jeans and sweatshirt, in his thirties – was trying to stop one of those vehicles that pull trolleys back to their home when they've been left on the platform. He was hanging onto the last trolley – pulling it back and pushing it from side to side. The driver, feeling something wasn't right, thought he'd hit someone and stopped. When he realised this was not the case, he drove on, with the young man glaring at him. The man then made a final run at the snaking line of trolleys and fell off the last one, turned abruptly and walked off into the dusk. It was five o'clock in the evening. Was he drunk? Was he trying to say something? Was it a cry for help? Is this English humour?

Pondering these questions, I sat on a bench in Victoria Street outside the station. I had an appointment with a cabinet minister in the nearby Department for Work and Pensions. I was early so I sat and waited. Big mistake. A man demanded money. Really demanded it: with malice. In Washington, there are beggars in the streets but most of them are polite. The panhandler outside the BBC office on M Street was rather pally – I used to bump fists with him every day. If he threatened me, or anyone, he'd be carted off.

But here in Hogarth's London, I am the one who must run. It strikes me as ironic – as I enter the relative safety of the Department for Work and Pensions – that no one in this building is armed. In a city way more dangerous than Washington – a city stuffed full of desperate characters – the guard at the door has nothing more than a pencil with which to defend himself. As you say in America: good luck with that.

As I mentioned at the beginning of the book, when I came home from America I wasn't expecting Britain to be easy. I knew that valet parking would soon be a distant memory. I knew that wide open spaces, proper vistas without houses or silly Stone

Age-style drawings of men with improbably large appendages, do not exist in the English countryside. I knew that Downing Street was as shabby as the White House is chic.

But nothing prepared me for the booze. Sometimes it seems as if everyone here is drunk. Now, here I should add an important proviso: perhaps it's me that's changed, not my country; when I lived here before leaving for the US, it is possible, I suppose, that everyone was drunk *but I didn't notice*. Perhaps I was too drunk myself. But live in Washington DC for the best part of ten years, and it becomes the most striking feature of the return to this side of the pond: America is sober, Britain is legless.

On a train, a group of people sat behind me and (I do not exaggerate) discussed for a full hour, London to Oxford, the various ways in which they had been sick. They were like Eskimos with snow: familiarity had bred a rich language to describe the subject. Subtle changes of colour, lumps, vomit venues: nothing was off-limits. Why should it be? This was a big part of their lives.

In America this conversation, among twenty-somethings on their way home from work, would be inconceivable, would it not? American college students drink. American drunks drink. But regular folk leading regular lives do not drink to excess. Biologists tell us that one of the attributes that separate humans from the rest of the animal kingdom is a sense of disgust. Animals lick their own sick. Humans recoil from it. Except in England on the train home.

One of the effects of this sobriety is to make the American equivalent of an English market town oddly peaceful in comparison. I am not claiming that America has no problems with booze among the young or among the general population at home behind the white picket fences, but when it comes to public drunkenness and the crime associated with it, mainstream middle-class America escapes the kind of scenes of puke-smelling, fist-filled mayhem that John Humphrys described for the *Today* programme recently after a night out in his home town of Cardiff.

When I lived in America and met Brits over on holiday, their comments were a constant refrain: "Wow, it seems so much gentler than we thought." Well, that's because it's sober. And let's face it, there are plenty of aspects of American life that are far more violent than ours, from capital punishment to relaxed gun ownership, to a deeply held belief (even after the experiences of recent years) that war is a legitimate and useful tool of foreign policy. America was created in violence and, fuelled by old-time religion, still has an occasional hankering for a shoot-out. But with booze in check, ordinary people in ordinary places can go about their lives unmolested. It still annoys me that my mum, during the last few years of her life, could not walk the streets of the city of Bath at night. Bath, of all places! Hardly the roughest of English cities. And not peopled by murderers of old ladies either. But at night it was infested with enough drink-filled yobbishness to make it unsafe for frail folk to go home from the cinema.

And yet... part of me, the English part perhaps, secretly rather enjoys boozed-up Britain. Talking to my wife the other day about why our first year back here had been 100 per cent more wonderful than we thought it would be, we both agreed that part of the problem with life in America was, well, *the sobriety!*

An example: quite early on in our Washington adventure, we were asked to a party by a very senior and well-known CNN correspondent. The beau-monde of the Washington broadcasting scene would be there. We turned up expecting sophistication. They were drinking punch. "Well, alright, just one glass," we said, fully intending to have ten. It looked a touch lethal – the colour of cherryade and served in large glasses. Lips touched liquid. It was all we could do not to spit it out. It *was* cherryade.

There was no booze. We were at a party with some of the most knowledgeable and well-connected and successful people in Washington and they were drinking cherryade. Somehow the whole event felt babyish. When a conjurer came in to entertain us (seriously!) and managed to take people's watches off without them realising, we were past caring. In Britain our kids would be beyond this stuff – and on the drink in some cases – in their teens, but in sober, temperance America it's what passes for a good time.

This memory led to a deeper and more worrying thought: did we really have anything at all in common with any of the people we had thought were our American friends? Had the whole thing been just a little too goody-two-shoes? Had those great fun evenings with Hank and Jo-Anne (names changed to protect the very innocent) actually been, at the deeper level of the soul, unsatisfying and shallow and uptight in a manner that allowed for no real connection to take place? Getting tipsy with friends, one of the great British pastimes, is perhaps a more important part of a well-lived life than we had realised.

There is also in America your weird cultural history of actually fearing alcohol. The disastrous legacy of the failed effort to ban it completely is the peculiar relationship between modern Americans and booze. I remember Stanley McChrystal, the boss of NATO forces in Afghanistan till he was sacked for "dissing" Barack Obama, telling me that one of the first things he was going to do when he got to Kabul was ban drinking in the officers' mess. At the time of this revelation, we were both standing at a bar near the Pentagon with beers in our hands. The idea that such relaxation, without drunkenness, could be acceptable when work is at hand is very difficult for many Americans to grasp. Stanley was having a drink because he was resting. When he went to work he was dry.

A friend who worked for Rupert Murdoch's Sky News in Washington confirmed this approach. To get to his bureau he had to walk through the Fox News office – and to be friendly on his first day he called out that anyone who fancied a drink should come with him. It was lunchtime. He might as well have told the Fox folk that he was a socialist transvestite. He was worried, he told me later, that they were going to call the cops.

The truth is that I am, as you Americans say, conflicted. I am revolted by the booziness of Britain but comforted as well. The other day, our sports presenter Gary Richardson came into the *Today* studio at 7.25 to do the sport carrying a glass of white wine. I didn't bat an eyelid. Actually, it turned out to be apple juice but what the heck: we are home! And feeling tipsy with delight...

And returning to Britain reminds me that the face America shows to the outside world, while sober in the extreme, is often oddly and unnecessarily hostile. Customs officials in the UK greet visitors face to face. I am sure there are some horrible ones among them but the general intention is to be civil. Even those passengers subjected to the greatest scrutiny are met initially by a person into whose eyes they can stare. Not so in America. The signs at Washington Dulles Airport speak of welcome, and the movie you watch while you wait in the hour-long queue to be seen speaks of homely America, but when you get to the front, the homeliness is replaced by something else: let's call it an abundance of caution. The immigration officials tend to be former military men – they are usually men – of a somewhat prickly disposition. They are armed; each one of them carries a pistol. Why? Any dangerous passengers would presumably have revealed themselves on the plane, not waited for the arrivals lounge.

Even the woman barking orders at the queue is armed. The truth, of course, is that they are not expecting to use the weapons – the queues are much safer than they would be at Victoria Station – but everyone with any kind of crowd-control authority in America tends to carry a gun. It is not really meant to be threatening, and not many Americans would give it a second thought, but the image is not friendly. Nor is the physical set-up for your passport check: the official is higher than you and surrounded by a steel-framed cubicle. I have met some quite amiable ones in my time, though generally when the talk gets to politics, as it does when they ask what I do for a living, their views are more Kansas than San Francisco. They are primarily there to keep bad guys out rather than let good guys in.

In both Europe and America, let's face it, the threat of violence in the modern age is low. When Hogarth really was prowling the streets of London, or when the Wild West was being won, it was commonplace. Now it's not. But efforts to parry what violence there is, whether that violence is organised or the result of individual human malice, diverge with the Atlantic. In America the forces of authority are ready for a fight and in some respects I think that makes America a rather more peaceful place to live. And yet that very readiness for a fight is tiresome and reminds you constantly of danger, real or exaggerated, around every corner, in every airport. Perhaps the British way is best, where jovial policemen chase the hooligans, the crowd cheers enigmatically, and on Victoria Station, it's every man for himself.

Chapter Eight

THERE IS A reckless energy in American public life, an energy that speaks of daring and winning, an energy that leaves the English in the shade. You saw it with Stanley McChrystal, the ill-fated head of the NATO mission in Afghanistan, who crashed and burned in 2010 after inviting a journalist from *Rolling Stone* on a drunken weekend jaunt to Paris. As I mentioned in the last chapter, Stanley was very sober on duty but on this occasion, it seemed, not so sober off duty. In Paris, he let his guard slip. It was a moment of madness but not out of character; it was in fact a moment of madness in a life full of such moments, an American life packed with bravado and not always quite as thought through as it might have been. Before he went to Afghanistan, appointed by the incoming President Obama to shake up the effort and define and execute victory, I visited the General in his Washington home.

In his sitting room there was a severed arm.

I noticed it immediately; I am, after all, a trained observer. And although I am also a pretty broad-minded fellow, in my limited experience of life, severed arms and sitting rooms do not necessarily go together. But nobody around me mentioned it. I was with his Pentagon minders waiting to interview the great man, and we made small talk about the Washington weather: already warming up, we agreed.

I cracked. "What's with the arm?"

I should explain that the severed arm was sticking out of the kind of ornate frame you might choose for a watercolour. The arm looked real – like a prosthetic limb. On closer inspection the oddity was compounded: in the hand there was a mobile phone.

The General entered, and explained: "The guys were fooling around. We went out to kill a sheik who had only one arm and we ended up getting the false arm but nothing else. That's not it," he adds, with a slight hint of wistfulness, "they just mocked that up for the joke. The phone was what gave his position away."

Stanley McChrystal was quite a character. In some respects he was out of central casting: big, with fierce eyes and weather-beaten skin. He looked every bit as fit as a Hollywood version of a special forces soldier. He ate one meal a day.

"That's not very good for you, is it?" I ventured.

"It's good for me."

When the General speaks, it's not a bark – this soldier has not seen a parade ground for many a long year – but a self-assured drawl. His voice is so quiet, in fact, that I have to strain to catch his words.

But it's worth the effort. America's military is often characterised as being more brawn than brain. In the past, some snooty Brits have suggested that Americans cannot really manage low-intensity wars because they're so wedded to their drones and nukes and kit. Literally, and metaphorically, they don't know when to take their helmets off, speak the local language, listen and learn.

Stanley McChrystal knew. The General was not an expert in counter-insurgency, nor did he claim to be. But he did know something about surgical strikes and the speedy use of human intelligence (and the signals sent out by mobile phones). He had a history of using massive force to great effect.

In Iraq (where the one-armed sheik got away), McChrystal is credited with killing dozens of key members of the insurgency. Until 2008 he led the Joint Special Operations Command, a shadowy group of soldiers and spies given the task of killing, capturing or otherwise neutralising senior members of Al Qaeda. Their biggest hit was Abu Musab al-Zarqawi, Al Qaeda's leader in Iraq. But he was far from the only target and far from the only scalp. There is a view that the success of the military surge in Iraq was due much more to the activities of General McChrystal's men than to the sheer number of boots on the ground.

And let us be plain: under his watch there were also allegations that those who were not killed were mistreated – tortured even – when brought back to base. He denies it but the allegation hangs around his neck.

He was certainly involved at every level in the operations he directed. At one of our meetings before he left for Afghanistan, I asked the General how close he had been to the nitty-gritty of soldiering in Iraq. His response spoke of his dedication to his art:

"I went out once a week with the guys. If they were going to pick someone off I liked to go along to keep in touch. They hated it, having me to look after!"

I doubted the last bit. They may have hated it, his men, but not because the General was a drag on their effort. Far from it: this man had standards and woe betide a junior officer who didn't match them.

When German NATO troops called in an air attack on stolen oil-filled tankers during his time in command, which killed a number of civilians in the process, McChrystal had trouble raising some of his European colleagues on the phone. It turned out they were having a drink in the officers' mess. No longer: drinking in all NATO establishments in Afghanistan was quietly banned.

As I've said, it's not that the General is teetotal, but that he was in Afghanistan on business. Focus was his thing. This is the American way. There is something about the American character that rolls up its shirtsleeves and ticks off tasks. It is not unthinking, this drive, but it does lead to an other-worldly relentlessness. A British friend who went to Harvard remembers a trip he and his classmates took to China. While having a drink on the plane out, they decided that they would speak the Mandarin they were learning – and only Mandarin – once they woke to get off their night flight. My friend woke up a few hours later, having long forgotten this champagne-fuelled pact. His friends had forgotten nothing. Solemnly, they reached for their bags and assisted each other with the boarding cards, speaking only Mandarin. The British chap realised that when it came to seriousness of purpose, he would always be a loser at his chosen university.

But the flip side of this seriousness of purpose is an ability to go off the rails with quite spectacular, Roman-candle like luminosity. Poor Stanley McChrystal managed it with his *Rolling Stone* interview, which saw him summarily fired by the slow-to-anger Obama. F. Scott Fitzgerald's famous dictum that there are no second acts in American lives is most often quoted today as an example of grandiose falsehood. Of course there are second acts: America is full of reinvention, revivification, is it not? Well, it is, but those picking up the pieces after a disaster are often the later generations. People get busted in America. They fly so high and fall so far that the wreckage, to use the old plane crash cliché, is spread over a wide area. F. Scott Fitzgerald had a point.

In a sense Obama himself fits into this category. His campaign for office was the most spectacular success in recent American history. He overcame hurdles of race and politics and personality to seize the presidency. He raised staggering sums of money. The American system allows such triumphs. A friend of mine – a French commentator – is fond of telling his countrymen that there are two necessities if you are to stand for high office in France. First, you must be known. Secondly, you must stand. In Britain it is the same; because of the lack of primaries our politicians must be stewed in the juices of Westminster before finally becoming famous and truly powerful. In America the opposite is the case. First, you must stand. Secondly, you need to become known. This encourages – in all aspects of American life – an approach that suggests possibilities before it fears dangers. An approach that juts out the chin and puffs up the chest before searching for the umbrella and asking the insurer whether you are covered.

But the corollary of this boldness is the fact that Americans can fall on their faces and not really, truly, ever get up again. Take Obama. He is – in spite of being of mixed race – America's first black president and his presidency has been a disappointment to many of his most ardent supporters because he has failed to transform the nation as he had promised. That is the epitaph. Nothing he does or says will really outlive that simple fact (or semi-fact). Just as Reagan won the Cold War, or Bush senior messed up the economy, or Bush junior invaded Iraq, Obama will be left in the minds of future Americans as a piece of graffiti that contains the word black and the word disappointment. His second term could be a success. His healthcare reforms could eventually bed down in a way that produces grudging respect. But the early years will always mark him. In Britain we do not do this. Non-partisan Brits will look back on Lady Thatcher with a genuinely more nuanced view. The folk memory points out her failures and her successes, just as it points out those of Blair and Cameron/Clegg. We British have an intuitive grasp of the warp and weft of life – and perhaps a limited expectation of success and transformation. We are willing to see progress made and lost and regained, as we see the tides pushing the waves up a pebbly beach and taking them down again. It is noisy, sometimes spectacular, but always ultimately futile. The British politician Enoch Powell's famous dictum that all political careers end in failure is truer in Britain than it is in the United States. Powell's dictum was a flattening one; it reminds us that we are all – even the grandest of us – heading for the same destination. In America, some careers actually end in success – think Reagan or Roosevelt – and the overriding view is that they have been, on balance, a triumph. So when you talk failure in American politics you do not necessarily accept the Powell view that you are not talking about anything unusual. To fail in America, in politics or in any other area of life, is really to fail. The excuse that Powell provides – everyone fails – is not available to you. The second act, in which everyone and everything is levelled, is not played in the American theatre.

Which leaves those of us who count ourselves as your friends wondering about how America will cope with the relative decline of her prestige and power that the next few decades will surely bring. American energy is devoted to winning, not taking part. It is going to be frustrating when other nations, and potentially other political systems, seem to be getting ahead, leading the world, setting the bar. The big question – and here is where we are so utterly different from you – is that of co-operation and pooled sovereignty. We are used to it. England, in the post-Falklands world, is more or less relaxed with the idea that if we do big things in the future we will do them with others. Our aircraft carriers, literally and metaphorically, have no jets to fly off them. In our dealings with everyone, friend and foe, there will be an element of compromise. We were very proud of the Olympic Games we put on in 2012 and to a large extent we did this alone, but in most of our endeavours we are in cahoots with others. America is not. It seems to me that Americans – most Americans – seriously believe that the founding fathers gave them the gift not just of constitutional independence but also of permanent freedom to act in accordance with the desires of the nation, irrespective of the opinions of lesser folks with lesser political systems. Nothing exemplifies this better than the fact that America is incredibly difficult to pin down when it comes to international treaties. American presidents often sign them but the Senate, whose job it is to ratify them and pass them into American law, quite frequently simply refuses. From the League of Nations to the International Criminal Court, America has a tradition of standing alone.

Many friends of America wonder why this nation, whose fundamental judgements are often perfectly in line with those of reasonable people elsewhere, cannot bring itself to take part in world society, to *play nice*, as you teach your children. After all, many of the institutions of the modern world were set up by America. The UN is in New York, not Beijing.

But this is where the differing psychologies – ours and yours – can be instructive. You have to look at what the English have internalised in the way of angst and failure and struggle. Or what the Americans have not had to cope with. You are not made like us. Your house is not falling down. You are still building, you want to think. The sun is still rising, you want to think. Tomorrow should be better than today, you want to think. To expect a people who want to believe these things, who have them at the core of their beings, to be cool about decline is to be unrealistic at best. The Wikileaks controversy of 2010 demonstrated the difficulties America is having in coming to terms with the new world order. On the one hand, Hillary Clinton's State Department was determined to keep ahead of the pack and believed that it had a right to do so; the instruction revealed by Wikileaks that American diplomats should steal biometric data from senior UN staff is evidence of a mindset that is, to put it mildly, interestingly old-fashioned in its pursuit of national self-interest. And yet, at the same time, Wikileaks revealed American behaviour that was perfectly, indeed naively, collegiate and mindful and respectful of the new order. In Yemen, for instance, the pretence that the local government was attacking terrorists (when in fact it was American missiles) was sensitively, and probably sensibly, arranged by General Petraeus, then head of local US forces. America did not rush in like a bull in a china shop. America thought about what to do; consulted as well. The entire picture to emerge from the Wikileaks dump hardly suggests that America is out of control; in fact, rather the opposite.

Then in 2011 came Egypt and Libya and the rest. And for America, a D-Day of sorts. An opportunity to storm some new beaches and – stretching the analogy a bit, but only a bit – having helped to win the peace, to secure a role in managing the post-war reality. After the Second World War it was known as the Truman Doctrine: President Truman vowed to fight to keep Greece and Turkey, and, later, all of Western Europe, free of communism and he did it by fair means and foul, with money and friendship and the occasional dirty trick to keep legitimate Communist parties in Italy and elsewhere on the hop. And so it might prove to be with America and Islamist forces in the modern Middle East. Except that America's desire to storm the beaches in 2011 has been pretty negligible. Its zest for the fight has deserted it, even though zest for fights is one of the things that – as I point out elsewhere – defines America. The weakest part of Barack Obama's speech in Westminster Hall in 2011 was the section that dealt with the Arab uprisings. It seemed to suggest some kind of ownership of them but didn't really back this claim up with practical promises of real help. This, then, is not a happy situation.

At a vital moment during the tense negotiations that led up to the UN Security Council resolution on Libya, a friend of mine who is a senior US diplomat received a text on his secure office phone. Excusing himself from the table, he found a place where he could not be overlooked and brought the message onto the screen.

"We need more rinse aid," it said.

It was his wife hoping he might be able to concentrate on two things at once.

The pressure she exerted on her husband is directly analogous to the pressures on the modern American world-view. Can you sort out the rinse aid at the same time as sorting out the world? Does the rinse aid get bought if money and time and effort are being spent in places where they don't even have dishwashers? Should you make sure the rinse aid is bought even at the expense of your other priorities?

Set aside for a minute the fact that President Obama was in charge as the Middle East burst into political life – the challenge was not just for him and the response was also a wider affair. This was about America and its view of its place in the world. The indispensable nation – as a former secretary of state called it – looked on from the sidelines as the Egypt crisis unfolded. At first America denied that President Mubarak was in trouble. Then they decided he was and needed to go. In Libya America decided that military action was "loose talk" and then engaged in it anyway a week or two later – then pulled away and let other nations get on with it. None of this looked very joined up. Critics of President Obama admonished him personally for this indecision, if that is what it was. But perhaps the blame needs to rest with the whole nation. The population was utterly torn over the whole Arab uprising. Not just torn between left and right, or interventionists versus non-interventionists, but torn inside minds as well; struggling to work out whether America's interest in cheap oil trumped her interest in freedom, whether supporting democracy in the Middle East might lead to longer-term threats to democracy in the West. But above all, America was unsure about what its role should be in a world in which a changed relationship between Washington and every other capital was a given. Does it make sense in the second decade of this century to do things that upset the Brazilians (who abstained on the UN Security Council resolution authorising the Libya action)? The question would have sounded ludicrous a few years ago, but now, in the age of relative decline, the age of the rise of new powers, it does not seem so silly.

So what should America do? The polls showed no great thrust of opinion one way or the other. The prominent Republican Newt Gingrich managed to argue both ways with equal vehemence – that America should get stuck in on the side of freedom, and then that the fighting in Libya was a travesty because the US had no vital interests in the region.

One well-known Washington intellectual told me at the time that Barack Obama had promised change but actually delivered the foreign policy of Brent Scowcroft, the famously unsentimental and realistic National Security Adviser of the first President Bush. He did not mean this as a compliment, but many Americans might have agreed with a shrug of the shoulders; America, in other words, was embracing a new reality, a new normal, in which the nation, by choice, would look to a tradition that has always been represented in its top echelons – the tradition of caution and even isolationism in foreign affairs – and accentuate that tradition by giving it a new and central post-war importance.

The painfulness of this debate was obvious for all to see at the beginning of 2011. Barack Obama maintained his customary cool – even going on a visit to South America while US forces were first in action over Libya – but the nation fretted about whether it was doing too little or too much. The French and (it was claimed) the Qataris led the way – propelled into world leadership roles by America's unwillingness to take the position that its people have become used to adopting. The French? Really? Almost nobody in America could place Qatar on a map. Why were they leading this operation? Who were they?

As the CNN political analyst Gloria Borgia put it:

> When the President says… "We should not be afraid to act – but the burden of action should not be America's alone," we get it. But we also start wondering: What happens if we're not driving the car? We always drive the car. Truth is, we like to drive. And when we're not driving, we think it's easy – even likely – for the coalition to veer off course. So here's the conundrum: we don't want to go it alone. Yet we're not sure we trust others to take the lead.

As the sand continues to swirl around the Middle East, it is too easy to see America's discomfort and apparent diffidence at key moments as being a function of the Obama presidency. It is undoubtedly the case that this President is more open to rumination than many previous occupants of the Oval Office – he promised as much when he campaigned and he has been as good as his word. But to suggest that it is all about Obama is to miss, perhaps, a key moment in modern history. America has reached a point where the urge to drive the car, the urge to lead, has run up against the reality of a new world order in which other nations are on the rise, and in which America itself feels unsettled and unconfident about its domestic affairs. It is worth pointing out that Washington – for all the talk of decline – was able to get the Libya action going while still heavily committed in Afghanistan. The military might of America – the cruise missiles and the planes and the sheer logistical majesty of its massive military machine – was still very much on show in Libya at the start of the operation; indeed, one wonders whether it really could have happened at all without the Americans being there, and ready to press the start button.

But having said that, the picture that emerges politically from recent events is of a giant rethinking of America's behaviour. This rethink – which is not yet over and must encompass at least one more change of presidency to become anything like permanent – affects America's relationship with the whole of the outside world, but more importantly, it affects its relationship with itself – the understanding that you Americans have of who you are. My sense is that hesitancy over Libya, diffidence and dithering in foreign affairs, comes not from the difficulties encountered around the world but more profoundly from a sense that all is not well at home. Americans, like Britons, are having to come to terms with the long-term aftermath of an economic calamity and a consequent loss of power.

However your depression in the face of decline is far more intense that ours. Part of this is psychological: you are not used to being in this place. But part of it too is brought on by a horrible realisation that you might be even worse off than we Europeans because you do not have a governing structure capable of dealing with the needs of the times. American government is in serious trouble and is troubled by that trouble, as the journalist Mort Zuckerman put it:

> We still possess the most appealing popular culture and public values, as well as the most innovative and competent business culture. American exceptionalism endures. But we must confront our dysfunctional and profligate government. America was founded on the principle of creating a better life for our children and grandchildren. We can do it. We aren't doing it.

In an article for *US News and World Report*, written shortly after the midterm elections of 2010, Zuckerman phrased it like this:

> The supreme confidence, national pride, and sense of achievement that marked the nation through its first 200 years have been transformed into a mood of doubt...
>
> Even the wealthiest and most highly educated are anxious at the decline of America's competitiveness. We seem unable to produce new generations of qualified leaders in the fields of science and technology. Our government has been incapable of addressing the nation's problems rationally and constructively. We are haunted that the world is catching up with America; the sense of uniqueness and self-esteem that has been a part of our national character since our founding – and has been amplified since World War II – is steadily eroding.

But the psychology of your country is still different and still out of line with our British post-imperial approach to world affairs. The reckless energy is still there at the heart of the American world mission. Can we help you cope with it? Run it off, perhaps, as one does with a toddler? This approach is doomed, as is every other effort at patronising Americans. There has to be a better way; a way that grasps the essence of America and works with it, respects it, allows it the space it needs to live and breathe.

You Americans, to be fully functioning, must be optimistic. Sometimes we foreigners forget how important it is to your peace of mind. Take the Heroic Imagination Project at Stanford University. Its website informs us:

> It's true. The world is indeed a dangerous place, and inhumane behavior – whether extraordinary evil or an individual act of cruelty – is unfortunately pervasive. But it is often entirely avoidable if only we trust ourselves to speak up, to call attention, to act responsibly. Why, then, is it so very difficult for the vast majority of us to take action in a crisis? What leaves so many people silent and paralyzed in the face of injustice or physical peril? Is heroic behavior a rare exception to the norms of human nature? We at the Heroic Imagination Project believe the answer is absolutely not. We believe heroism can be learned by example and reinforced with practice. Our programs are designed to inspire heroism in ordinary people and teach them to make wise and effective decisions when heroic opportunities arise.

The *Today* programme arranged an interview with the boss of the project, a psychologist of some repute, but eventually we decided that the piece was unusable. It was not exactly the content, which was interesting enough. It was not the arguments and ideas or the accent that made us drop it: it was just that, well, the whole thing seemed so, umm, American! Culturally, we decided, it simply could not run; it would be regarded by the *Today* audience as utter gobbledygook. It was not a case of potentially broadening minds or introducing foreign and difficult concepts. No: this was a category error, as the philosophers put it; where the two parts of the equation (the *Today* audience and the Heroic Imagination Project) simply could not meet because they were so utterly, profoundly, logically (ontologically!) separate. The idea of teaching heroism is not going to take off in Britain. In America it would be universally accepted: *way to go*!

This is why you Americans get so hurt when people are not heroic. Ronald Reagan, in his first inaugural speech, referred to America as "a living, breathing presence, unimpressed by what others say is impossible, proud of its own success; generous, yes, and naive; sometimes wrong, never mean, always impatient to provide a better life for its people in a framework of a basic fairness and freedom". I still recognise his America – viewed, perhaps, with the generosity of an affectionate outsider – but many Americans frankly do not. You still want to think in these terms, but faced with the evidence, you find it difficult.

What does the future hold for you and how can we help, or hinder, the process of America's coming to terms with the modern world? It is worth being honest with ourselves first on the subject of debt. It is a fact that America's greatness (and Britain's) was created by debt, or a willingness to use debt as a tool, allied to prudence about finding ways of paying back that debt in the long term. Without debt the English-speaking peoples would be much diminished as forces in world history. In *God and Gold*, the historian Walter Russell Mead points out that the century that really created the modern dominance of the US – the nineteenth century – saw America having to borrow money in every year: "The American nation was a debtor nation throughout the nineteenth century; it was a much greater and richer country after one hundred years of debt." The same was the case – as every economic historian would accept

– for Britain in the key periods of our history when our power was being entrenched: we borrowed, paid it back and borrowed some more.

So what is the fuss about? There are two reasons why modern American government debt – the cumulative total of each year's difference between what is spent and what is raised in taxes – is such a massive threat. The first is that the actual sums – as a percentage of national wealth – are very high. Within a few years America is likely to owe roughly the same as it is worth. In Britain the figure that so spooked the incoming coalition government in 2010 was that our debt had reached around 60 per cent of our wealth. So America's debt is very high. It has been high before – around the time of the Second World War – but not nearly as high in any peacetime period. The second reason why American debt might be so catastrophic in the modern era is that the baby boomers are retiring and are about to put unprecedented strain on the system of benefits – medical and social – that is aimed at older Americans. These payments to these people have been guaranteed and must be made. So if the Chinese decide to lend less to America and the dollar interest rate rises, America faces a period of potentially catastrophic austerity.

Even if the Chinese stay friendly, it has been suggested that by 2025 America will raise only enough in taxes to cover entitlement spending (unemployment benefits, health spending for the elderly and disabled, pensions etc) and interest payments; everything else, from defence to transport to security to energy to education, will have to be borrowed money.

This America, the America described by the facts just mentioned, is a very different place to the jolly(ish) nation we foreigners think of today. The potential for domestic strife is huge as is the potential for complete withdrawal from the outside world. Getting on for a quarter of US debt is held by the Chinese government. What if China, facing its own domestic pressures, decides to go rogue and slash its dollar holdings? What if China simply pulls the rug from under the US? As one commentator has put it, with reference to America's continuing defence of Taiwan from a Chinese takeover: "Chinese central bankers could prove more dangerous than Chinese Admirals." In other words, the threat of economic disaster could well persuade America to ditch allies and ditch commitments. And it is not just the Chinese. Who will listen to the US if they know that the nation is in crisis and cannot afford to pay its way? American power will be reduced in practical reality and its example – the shining city on the hill – will also be tarnished since the system you have long told us is the best turns out to have ruined you.

But it is not just the debt. It is the failure to be able to deal with it. Here the UK shows the way and America is left flailing in our wake. Let me be very clear here: I am not talking about the actual policy adopted by the coalition government. I am not suggesting that they were right or they were wrong to go down the road they chose. Nor am I suggesting that Barack Obama was right or wrong to take the actions he took in the first few years of his presidency. My point is a deeper one: in Britain we were still capable of taking those decisions. Our political system was flexible enough and open enough for a reasonably honest debate (at least post-election) of what our options might be and what courses of action were available.

No such debate is possible in America. One of the great features of modern American life is the utter debasement of your politics. People focus on the language used and the recklessness of the arguments – and in a later chapter I explore the possible reasons for this and whether British broadcasting rules might be part of the reason we escape such nastiness – but the really fundamental problem is not the roughness of the language or the craziness of the tobacco-chewing cousin-marrying folks: it is the inability of Americans, including clever, well-educated, sophisticated Americans, to engage in a real debate about what options their nation has.

An example is Sarah Palin's home state, Alaska. When I say Alaska, what comes to mind? Snow probably. Frozen wastes. Animals. Hunting. Rugged stuff and rugged folks – millions of miles from Washington and millions of miles from the cosseted lives of Americans who live in the suburbs of the big cities. Wrong. As the commentator Anne Applebaum put it:

> The hypocrisy at the heart of the [Republican] party – and at the heart of American politics – is at its starkest in Alaska. For decades, Alaskans have lived off federal welfare. Taxpayers' money subsidizes everything from Alaska's roads and bridges to its myriad programs for Native Americans. Federal funding accounts for one-third of Alaskan jobs. Nevertheless, Alaskans love to think of themselves as the last frontiersmen, the inhabitants of a land "beyond the horizon of urban

clutter," a state with no use for Washington and its wicked ways.

The unreality exists too in the realm of guns. I have written before about how peaceful America often seems as a place to live; although it has more murders than other civilised nations, it has less minor crime. I do not think that taking America's guns from their owners (not a realistic proposition anyway) would necessarily make the nation better. It would save some lives for sure; but guns are too tightly woven into the fabric of American life for their non-existence to be contemplated. However, there is a complete fallacy at the heart of what many Americans believe about guns and this fallacy is part of the depressing myopia that poisons American political debate. The fallacy is this: that guns are what guarantee American freedom: of religion, of conscience, of daily life. The truth is that if you look around the world at societies that are gun-infested or gun-protected (take your pick), there is quite obviously no link between personal possession of weapons and freedom. As *The Economist* put it, with admirable clarity and coolness, shortly after the infamous attack on a congresswoman in Arizona in 2010 in which a number of people, including a nine-year-old child, died:

> There is no link between individual ownership of firearms and democratic governance or civil rights and freedoms. The main determinant of guns per population member, as for cars per population member, is wealth. And yet, while the United States has the most guns per person in the world, the number two country appears to be Yemen, not usually considered a bastion of democracy or civil rights. Individual ownership of firearms is much higher in Saudi Arabia and Russia than in Britain; it is much higher in Pakistan than in India. The idea that individuals could use their private firearms to mount a serious challenge to government hegemony is only plausible in very weak states. When individuals, militia or criminal gangs foolishly attempt to directly challenge police or the National Guard in the United States, they are quickly overpowered, killed or arrested.

It's an important point, this. During my time in America I always felt that the British obsession with American gun crime was overblown – guns are part of America and most gun owners are decent peaceful people. But here is an uncomfortable fact. My old house at 3805 Windom Place has the zip code 20016, and I've discovered that since the Supreme Court relaxed gun ownership laws in Washington, one zip code above all others has accounted for a surge in gun-buying: 20016. This feels to me like a kind of madness. When I called on the neighbours recently, I pushed open their front door – they would not have thought to lock it. 20016 is one of the safest places to live *in the world*. Sometimes someone parks a car facing the wrong way – you are meant to park facing the direction of traffic – but this is the limit of local criminality. Nobody who has bought a gun in 20016 can possibly have done it out of a rational belief that he or she was reducing the risk of being attacked. So why did they? The reason is deeper and it seems to me – with my newfound detachment from American life – worrying. Americans have long convinced themselves of the falsehood that *The Economist* so tellingly debunks: that there is a link between guns and freedom at the level of society; that the more guns there are in the hands of individuals, the more difficult it would be for a dictator to take power. This is the freedom guaranteed by the second amendment to the constitution passed in 1791. And still the argument about gun control is an argument about what the amendment actually means. It is the wrong argument! The real argument should be whether civilised societies in the modern age are made safer by guns – but that argument is beyond America. So far beyond America that even Barack Obama, who cannot really be a friend of guns, has done precisely nothing to advance the agenda of those who would limit gun ownership. The debate on gun ownership in the US is skewed by the failure of those opposed to guns to state clearly and honestly the obvious truth: guns do not guarantee liberty in modern America. There may be all manner of reasons for keeping them but that really should not be one of them. It is a way of thinking similar to the Alaskans and their potty self-image as frontiersmen even while they suck at the teat of central government. But nobody in modern America can tell the Alaskans not to be so silly and nobody tells the National Rifle Association that either.

Barack Obama is as guilty here as any other politician. When gun ownership in Washington DC was an issue before the Supreme Court in 2008 (with the court being lobbied to allow greater gun rights), he kept quiet. He had little other choice. Because of the utterly false link in many American minds between guns and freedom, he would have been committing electoral suicide to speak out. He wanted to win in states where Democrats had as many guns as anyone else – states like Montana, where the Democratic Party Governor told me in no uncertain terms that he would never back any kind of limit on weapons: "For us, gun control is hitting what you shoot at!"

Did this change in 2012 at Sandy Hook school in Newtown CT? The horror of Sandy Hook – twenty little lives ended by a deranged gunman, and six teachers dead as well – will live forever in American history. Of that we can be sure. But its true impact – its effect on the nation – is less easy to predict. My own view – as a friendly foreigner respectful of American traditions and American exceptionalism – is that it might help to begin a long inter-generational process of breaking the link in American minds between freedom and guns in the modern world. In the end this would be much more useful than a new set of rules about how quickly people can reload their weapons or how easily they can buy them. The real challenge for America is to use these tragedies to allow reasonable decent thoughtful people on both sides of the argument to examine what guns are for. They are part of America's past but must they be part of the future? Are they necessary? Really necessary? In spite of all this mayhem? That is the discussion to have; forget the fussing about the meaning of the second amendment. Cut to the quick.

The point is vitally important to an understanding of modern American politics and the modern American crisis. Too many Americans have seriously lost touch with reality. Alaskans are not the only folks to have kidded themselves that they are living lives which, in reality, they are not. Your whole nation has rendered itself incapable of holding a proper debate about what to do regarding its debt because nobody really understands – or is capable of admitting – what the problem is and what the options are. There is no better example than tax. Nobody likes paying taxes but part of the solution to the financial crisis of recent years has got to be a rise in government income. No serious person on either side of the Atlantic disputes this. But there are very few serious people on the US side. It is pathetic to see Americans scrabbling around trying to fund their education system through sponsorship from fizzy drinks manufacturers, trying to fund their mental health services through state lotteries that contribute to the breakdown and misery the money is then spent alleviating. Tax avoidance – on a national scale – has somehow become part of the American self-image.

This is a historical nonsense. Throughout most of the twentieth century – the American century – national income tax levels were higher than they are now. American governments in the past have been able to raise the funds to build the nation and invest in its future. Now if you suggest a VAT for America (not a bad idea as it is a tax that can be collected easily and is difficult to avoid), you are painted as a wild-eyed socialist. Even plans to reduce the current 100-per-cent tax exemption for mortgage interest payments (100 per cent!) are hugely controversial. Taking a leaf out of your Alaskan neighbours' book, you refuse to grasp that you are massive consumers of government funds and they need to find the money from somewhere. True, there are some Americans who genuinely and intellectually coherently argue for a smaller state, but they are nowhere near a majority. Most Americans in the 21st century have come to see themselves as frontiersmen but they want to live the lives (particularly when they retire) of French civil servants. Dissonance is the mildest way of describing it. Utter barminess comes closer. And it infects all aspects of the debate on the choices available – because nobody is being really honest about what kind of a nation America is.

And the dishonesty allows both main political parties to avoid the tough choices they are forever talking about taking. This is how the economist Jeffrey Sachs sees it:

> The problem is America's corrupted politics and loss of civic morality. One political party, the Republicans, stands for little except tax cuts, which they place above any other goal. The Democrats have a bit wider set of interests, including support for health-care, education, training, and infrastructure. But, like the Republicans, the Democrats, too, are keen to shower tax cuts on their major campaign contributors, predominantly rich Americans. The result is a dangerous paradox. The US budget deficit is enormous and unsustainable. The poor are squeezed by cuts in social programmes and a weak job market. One in eight Americans depends on food stamps to eat. Yet, despite these circumstances, one political party wants to gut tax revenues altogether, and the other is easily dragged along, against its better instincts, out of concern for keeping its rich contributors happy.

Where do we come in? It seems to me that the debate about military approaches to world problems versus softer power needs to be upgraded and made more concrete. England needs to encourage America to be more honest about the kinds of economic choices available in the coming years and the kinds of implications they have for the world. English politicians need to encourage American politicians to understand that they can maintain their central position in the affairs of the planet *only* if they sort out their economy, and that has to start with sorting out their politics, regaining the ability to make choices, an ability vital to a proper functioning democracy.

You have to have a better understanding of your own history. Presidents Truman and Eisenhower both fought the Cold War with great vigour, yet both understood that economic strength at home was as vital as skirmishes in foreign lands. They improved science education and built highways. Today, that means concentrating on sorting out Mexico rather than Afghanistan or Libya, on addressing illegal immigration and boosting trade. It does not mean withdrawal from the outside world nor an end to involvement in foreign wars, but it does mean recognising that America's key contribution to the world is the example of its domestic self. America needs to get away from its foolish obsession with the language of its constitution and even with some of its certainties. The academic Samuel Huntington once referred to America as a "Tudor Polity": he meant that the patterns of government Americans prefer – decentralised and in constant opposition – are in fact modelled on sixteenth-century Britain, where power was diffuse and held by the Church, the Inns of Court, the barons and the municipal corporations as much as by the Tudor monarchs. Guys, seriously, this may not be the best way of approaching the new century! Perhaps our politicians need to be more honest in telling you Americans that you have to pull your socks up. It need not be a hectoring message or a condescending one; in fact it is the opposite of condescending since it recognises the indispensability of the world's richest nation. It is a message from a true ally – no longer wittering on foolishly about the nature of our relationship, but using our linguistic and cultural closeness to some real purpose.

Chapter Nine

YOU NEED TO understand how your use of language
upsets us because it tells you something about our
relationship – something about us and something
about you.

In my first week back in Britain presenting the *Today* programme, I glanced at the clock and announced to a bemused nation that it was "a quarter of eight".

Guys, relax. Suck it up. Enjoy. Or not... I can reveal exclusively that many people did not enjoy the moment or feel able to suck it up. They were unrelaxed for several days afterwards. (We say quarter to, not quarter of...)

American English – Americanisms generally – reduce otherwise reasonable, rational English folks to neuralgia and worse. "What's the weather going forward?" – to me a perfectly comprehensible question – would cause hernias in the *Today* office. Dudes, I remind them: "Y'all need to know that I spent eight years in the US, my children grew up there, and a subtle change in the language has kinda seeped in."

Part of me understands exactly why it can be so annoying to us English. We invented the confounded language, after all. We perfected it; our ancestors fought the wars and established the culture that made it such a worldwide force, so why should we see it barbecued and handed back with tomato sauce on top? What was wrong with it raw? The (normally) gentle and deeply cultured English journalist Matthew Engel put it like this in a piece in the *Mail on Sunday*:

> Old buffers like me have always complained about the process, and we have always been defeated. In 1832, the poet Samuel Taylor Coleridge was fulminating about the "vile and barbarous" new adjective that had just arrived in London. The word was "talented". It sounds innocuous enough to our ears, as do "reliable", "influential" and "lengthy", which all inspired loathing when they first crossed the Atlantic. But the process gathered speed with the arrival of cinema and television in the 20th Century. And in the 21st it seems unstoppable. The US-dominated computer industry, with its "licenses", "colors" and "favorites" is one culprit. That ties in with mobile phones that keep "dialing" numbers that are always "busy".
>
> My dictionary (a mere 12 years old) defines "geek" as an American circus freak or, in Australia, "a good long look". We needed a word to describe someone obsessively interested in computer technology. It seems a shame there was never any chance of coining one ourselves. Nowadays, people have no idea where American ends and English begins. And that's a disaster for our national self-esteem. We are in danger of subordinating our language to someone else's — and with it large aspects of English life.

But having lived for so long in America and having heard my children speak American and watched them make the transition back to English, I want to make the case that rather than apologising for messing up English English – as some Americans are still tempted to do in a kind of cultural cringe – you should be much more insistent that there is much to be loved about the idioms of the New World. It is not all about laziness. It enriches as well as simplifies our mother tongue.

English people tend to think of American English as a pointer to a lazier, quotidian future, in which a brainless homogeneity is achieved at the expense of rigour and linguistic crunch.

In American that might read: "We're all gonna talk the same."

But sometimes American English can surprise with its quaint, even dainty, formulations. When was the last time you were asked in England if you wanted a beverage?

A *what*? It's a perfectly good word and we all know what it means but in English English it would be an odd way of buying someone a drink. In America, beverages are served on every street corner. Dr Pepper anyone?

I grew to love too the term "person of colour" meaning black or dark-skinned individual. Barack Obama has used it to great effect when talking about the newly prominent Republican Party leader, John Boehner. We are both, the President says, *people of colour*. The joke, of course, was that Mr Boehner was a white man who lived in Ohio (where the sun don't shine) but had a skin tone that suggested the frequenting of tanning salons or fancy foreign holiday destinations – and neither is good for Republican credibility.

I must admit that some American English is too chintzy even for my New World tastes. I hate the inability of Americans, in polite society, to call a spade a spade. A letter complaining about my defence of American English on a radio programme years ago pointed out, quite reasonably, that the results of this daintiness can sometimes be utterly ludicrous. The example the letter-writer gave was a natural history programme she had seen in the US, in which a hippopotamus was said to be "going to the bathroom".

But still, when I hear my children speak American English, I cannot help but smile. Stern-faced people used to ask me and my wife about the efforts we were making to help our kids lose their accents. None, we would reply. They did it themselves and, to a large extent, along with the accents have gone the idioms.

But just occasionally one will appear, like a shot of Jack Daniels on a cold day. So although they speak like the Queen, they can still be heard announcing that they are "done" rather than "finished" or that their day at school was "regular". They still struggle a bit with English place names – Folkes*town* is my favourite – but generally they are good. Sorry, fine.

The obvious advantage of American English is that it is, to a much greater extent than English English, genuinely classless. There used to be a suggestion that Americans on the East Coast tended – mentally and linguistically – to bow the knee to the old nations of Europe; only Midwesterners were properly American. It is certainly true that fashionable New York accents from the 1950s sound oddly English. This is partly because they fancied themselves as the Eurotrash of the time and partly because they were simply a group of people who had lived in one geographic region for many years – other Americans were too new to their neighbourhoods to have any settled habits apart from godliness and a way with a Colt 45.

Those days are gone now and there is a wealth of American accents and language on the East Coast to put alongside the flat Midwestern, and of course the classic Southern drawl. Accents to Americans certainly suggest stuff. But never quite class stuff, in the British sense. Take the Southerner. He or she drawls. "Why?" becomes "Whaaaa?"; "nail" becomes "nay-eel". Instead of saying "going to" he says "fixin' to". And the language slows. And life slows. Is this lower class? No way. A Southerner might be suspected of being a hangover from *Gone with the Wind*, but his or her accent could put him or her up there in a starring role with the Rhetts and Scarletts, or down there with the slaves. You could not tell the difference from accent or from lexicon. And that is the same across the nation. Of course, educated Americans have more words at their disposal than do the uneducated. But the words used by all manner of folk will be far more similar than they are in Britain. And the head of state – be it George Bush or Barack Obama – will talk like the population. The Queen does not. After the announcement that Prince William's wedding day was to be a bank holiday, the papers were full of "day orf" headlines; how odd that the nation feels itself so utterly removed from the boss class that even the simplest word is pronounced differently. Sure, the Bushes mangled the language, but the language they were mangling was the same language that everyone else spoke. Do not misunderestimate the importance of this – to you and to us.

Did you Americans have to steal our language? It seems quite obvious to us now that you did; after all, most of the early settlers were from England. What could possibly persuade them to choose anything other than their mother tongue? Surely they never considered anything else? Actually, of course there is some suggestion that they did. In his masterly book *The American Language* (itself an effort to set out the case for the phenomenon it sought to describe), the great commentator H. L. Mencken mentions the hilarious (and possibly apocryphal) story of plans hatched during the revolution to abandon English as the national language for America and substitute Hebrew. Mencken adds that Greek was also reportedly considered but rejected on the grounds that "it would be more convenient for us to keep the language as it is, and make the English speak

Greek". Whatever: the passion for independence led to a loathing for English authority in all areas including, well, English. Noah Webster, of Webster's dictionary fame, said after the revolution that Americans should "seize the present moment, and establish a national language as well as a national government. As an independent nation our honor requires us to have a system of our own, in language as well as government".

And that language was already being put into use. When Ben Franklin was sent to France as America's first ambassador, shortly after the Declaration of Independence, he was instructed by Congress to employ "the language of the United States". Franklin worked hard on the project. But even these early zealots stopped short of real big change (as they might have put it) as proposed by "a Scotchman of the name of Thornton". This man, Mencken notes, "having settled in the new republic and embraced its *Kultur* with horrible fervor, proposed a new alphabet even more radical than Franklin's. This new alphabet included e's turned upside down and i's with their dots underneath. 'Di Amerike languids,' he argued, 'uil des bi az distint az de gevernment, fri from aul foliz or enfilosofikel fasen.'"

Enough already. It did not catch on. But "Americanism" did and the man who coined the term, John Witherspoon, did not mean it as a compliment. Witherspoon was a keen member of the Continental Congress and no friend of the English, but in matters of language he was anything but a revolutionary. Mencken quotes him thus:

> "I have heard in this country," he wrote in 1781, "in the senate, at the bar, and from the pulpit, and see daily in dissertations from the press, errors in grammar, improprieties and vulgarisms which hardly any person of the same class in point of rank and literature would have fallen into in Great Britain."

One of the great complaints by the English of the Americans concerned the clarity of the new language. Imagine: anyone could speak it. One magazine sniffed that in American English the speakers thought "one word as good as another provided its meaning be clear". Gettoutahere!

The inanity of the English attack is obvious from some of the words the early Disgusteds of Tunbridge Wells complained about. "Lengthy" was one. Do some English patriots still avoid it?

The other irony of this century's linguistic battle is that many of the words the Brits complained about (and still do) were actually English words that had been brought over on the *Mayflower* but then discarded by the flighty English. They were, in fact, more English than the English. They were proper. But the English had forgotten them. These orphan words had been adopted by the colonists and had prospered in the colonies – like little English refugees, they had taken flight in the New World and were thus resented back at home.

Other words flowed from you to us over the years. Backwoodsman is all-American. So is caucus. And squatter. Some Americanisms are born but never go anywhere – they wither on the vine even in their home country. Mencken gives "cars" for railway carriages. Just occasionally you still hear it but the universal usage of the mid-nineteenth century was gone by the late twentieth and never made it to England. Not that anything in language is dead for ever. Dude, Mencken suggests, was born in 1883 but was dead by 1895. In 2010, in an interview with President Obama, the great Jon Stewart caused a stir by calling the Commander in Chief "dude" – but the upset was caused by the familiarity; the word is everywhere. Will it ever come to Britain? I doubt it; there is something about its easy familiarity that we might find difficult to take on board. David Cameron might be Dave but he will never be dude.

Similarly, the word "lot" meaning a parcel of land is easy and useful (and my children still ask whether we are leaving the car in a lot) but is oddly lacking from English English. Lot probably comes from the fact that early land allocation in the US was conducted by drawing lots. In that respect it is all-American. Do we complain about "lumber"? Lumber used to mean discarded furniture (lumber room) but now, to most Brits, it means cut trees. Are we the less for this change? Another infestation that my family would like to claim credit for, if it ever comes off, is the use of "store" instead of "shop". In America, a shop is somewhere you leave your car (the machine-shop), and a store is where you shop. In England, that is not the case and I see no real chance that it will become the case, in spite of my efforts in south London. Matthew Engel himself admits: "Almost all the parts of a car have different names in America, yet there is no sign of hood replacing bonnet, or the trunk supplanting the boot." That's freedom, Matthew! We can name our own parts. And when we like them, we can keep them.

And then, there are subtleties: road haulage is a good one. U Haul is one of the great American brands; you use it when you want to escape and do that reinventing we mentioned in Chapter One. You gather up all your belongings and pack them in a van that attaches to the back of your car. On the side of it are emblazoned the words U Haul. In English English, the meaning is obvious – someone is hauling this stuff somewhere and that person is you. And yet the word haul to Americans means something more: it means to take something somewhere by a means of transport. Road haulage, to an American, is tautological. Now we rub along with this difference but it is there, unresolved, like so much else in our linguistic relationship.

Another favourite – and this one is mentioned by Mencken – is that in America you are "sick" but in England you are "ill". "Doctor, I am sick" (in spite of sickies and sick notes) is a statement you would not hear in England. But sick is the original Anglo-Saxon word. For some reason the Puritans decided it was too vulgar and changed to the old Norse "ill". In America you started with sick and decided (rough, tough folks that you were) to stick with it. Actually, Mencken thinks it was probably to do with their Bibles: the colonists had few other books and could see no obvious point in changing them to accommodate a different word.

"I guess" is my final choice. Here is Shakespeare:

Not all together; better far, I *guess,*
That we do make our entrance several ways.
Henry VI

You can't argue with the Bard.

I suppose, in fact, you can, but the argument seems to me a giant waste of time and energy, and one ultimately doomed to failure. Matthew Engel is left spluttering by the sheer size of the task he has set himself and readers of the *Mail on Sunday* in turning back the tide. He understands that this is no small challenge, and towards the end of one of his linguistic pieces, he offers the doleful view that "the most effective remedy would be the abolition of 24-hour news channels and breakfast TV, both American imports of no merit". Oh, Matthew, believe me, my man – it ain't gonna happen. I think American English is good English. I am proud that my children almost speak it. I wince when I see English accents used in

American TV to denote trustworthiness or quality. It's the final frontier folks: time to embrace your language.

Chapter Ten

THERE IS ANOTHER side to you and us. It has little to do with the broader questions of politics or society. It is smaller in scale than the rise of China or the size of the public debt or the future of education or the issue of gun control. It is removed from speeches made in Congress or the House of Commons. It is never on the front pages of the newspapers.

It is the internal psychological make-up of you Americans and us Brits; the lives not of the intellect but of the mind; the connections we make with our families and with ourselves. In the old days it would have been shrinks versus cold showers; stiff upper lips versus letting it all hang out. It is the cultural divide between us at the elemental level – the foundation level – of psychology.

I know something about this because I have myself lived what Americans consider to be the ultimate repressed English life. First, I went to boarding

Justin Webb

school, which only the weirdest Americans do. Secondly, I had a secret that I think I am probably right in saying most Americans could not in this day and age imagine keeping to themselves.

On the January 17th, 2010, at 4pm on a dull news day, the following piece was flashed by the Press Association news agency to its subscribers around the UK:

Embargoed to 0001 Tuesday January 18
14.32 – PA – BBC PRESENTER 'SECRET SON OF NEWSREADER'
By Anthony Barnes, Press Association

Radio 4 presenter Justin Webb has revealed for the first time he is the secret son of respected newsreader Peter Woods.

The Today programme host, 50, had no contact with his late father apart from a brief encounter at the age of six months and has kept his identity under wraps throughout his life.

Woods was a celebrated host of the BBC's flagship Nine O'Clock News and one of the great characters of his day. Famously, one BBC2 bulletin in the 1970s had to be faded out when he was audibly slurring his words. Webb has gone public about his father by writing about him for the first time in the new edition of Radio Times. Webb said he "buried" his father's identity in his mind to the extent he felt little connection and never considered getting in touch, even when he followed in the same career.

I was 50: just a few days past my birthday. From the moment I first knew – when I suppose I was five or six – to that day, I had told only my wife and (I think I remember rightly) one very discreet friend at university. My mother had told my parents-in-law, and her sister and brother also knew. That was it. A secret about the most fundamental facts of where I came from – who my father was – had been kept throughout my childhood and most of my adult life. Americans have secrets too but not, generally, of this kind. Americans share. With friends and – if they are relatively wealthy – with an entire industry of professional listeners. America is a nation devoted to what the medical folk call "talking therapies". It is, more than any other nation on earth, the home of exploration of the self.

Are we going in this direction in Britain? And if so, at what cost, and with what benefits?

A late-autumn day on the beach at Seaton in south Devon. It is desolate in a way that only the English seaside can manage. Gloomy overweight families, unaccountably late in their holidaymaking (waiting for the really cheap rates, perhaps?) sit vacant-eyed in fish and chip shops. The wind is cold and the pebble-dashed houses huddle back from the beach. People are boarding up, winterising. There is still ice cream but only the hardiest have the stomach for it.

On the beach – behind a slightly torn wind barrier – sit two figures. A mother and a son have made a nest among the pebbles. She's not yet old – perhaps in her forties – and he looks about ten or twelve. Why, when I see them, do I have the urge to stare? To walk up to them, to hug them both and tell them: "It can be ok! This life – this intense love and this gaping hole where a father should be – it can eventually give way to normality and a life happily lived."

We are visiting a relative and we have an hour to kill. To amuse my own children – who have not noticed the only other people on the beach – I go into the water. I have always enjoyed the shock of swimming in extreme cold – one day it may kill me but there are worse ways to go. My wife Sarah and our children laugh and toy with coming in themselves, then give up on the idea, but from the windbreak twenty yards away I notice a movement. The boy and his mother are coming down to the water's edge and the boy is ready to pull off his sweatshirt and come in himself. It is cold – very cold – but he is powered by something I recognise instantly as unstoppable. He wants to test himself against the elements and to do so in the presence of another man. He wants to get away from the comforting but cloying closeness with Mum and have a go at something painful – something from which a mother, any mother, would instinctively withdraw, but into which a father, any father, would plunge recklessly, knowing that half the fun of being male is contained in foolish plunges into all kinds of trouble.

For a few minutes we swim about, he and I. We exchange only a few words – he is not there to talk. We are buffeted by freezing waves; hit hard and smashed onto the stones. Eventually, worried I might actually have a heart attack and spoil the whole day, I get out and salute him. He waves. He looks radiantly, gloriously happy. And as I turn away I feel like crying.

Of course, I have no way of knowing whether they really were a mother and son with no father. Perhaps Dad was at home or at work. I could have misunderstood the whole thing. But I doubt it: I have antennae for these things. I am not the world's brightest, most emotionally intelligent being (my wife says) but I know a mother and son alone when I see them. I know them because I was in that team. I spent a whole childhood sitting on the beach hoping for a man to come along and take me for a dangerous swim. A whole childhood looking after Mum, loving Mum, but unsure about how this would end.

Incompleteness is a secret many English people keep. Sad, lonely childhoods are not, it is fair to say, entirely unusual. Plenty of successful people feel themselves driven through their lives by a sense of loss experienced while young, or simply by the spur of trying to escape from circumstances that were in some way desperate; a lack of love, or poverty, perhaps. Our early lives, thank goodness, do not shape us in ways that cannot be reordered later, and, sometimes, we manage to find ways of taking charge and using adversity to build firmer foundations for the future. We do it as adults but we often do it, almost unconsciously, as children.

Here is where it gets complicated in my case and in the cases of dozens of people who have written to me since I revealed that my father was Peter Woods. I grew up with a sense of longing and a sense of loss – actually there was a man in the house, Charles, whom my mother married when I was three or four, but he was mentally ill and cold and distant. He was never Dad. (My mother used to tell the story of how, when I was young, I asked her one day: "Where did we *get* Charles?") But this oddness was compounded by another.

I was always aware that there was something I knew about my life and could never reveal to others; something my mother had not exactly banned but talked of only with reluctance.

What I have found revealing about the kind notes and emails I received after I spoke out about my father, was quite how many told of similar secrets and the effects those secrets can have. Being brought up by Mum is generally looked back on – perhaps particularly by boys – as perfectly survivable. In fact, I think I read somewhere that the concentration of affection it entails can be regarded as a good thing – strong women can bring up strong men: Barack Obama is a shining example. But the secretiveness is less easy to chalk up as a potential plus.

Did you know your father? Well, no is the answer I used to give to acquaintances who enquired, I did not know him because he had left. Did you know anything about him: did you have any contact with him? That was trickier; do you have *contact* with someone if you watch them on the TV every night? I suppose you could argue that this is not contact as generally understood, but you begin to feel like Bill Clinton disputing – during the Monica Lewinsky affair – the meaning of the word "is". With this answer – I had no contact with him – I was in the realms of revealing so much less than the full truth that it was becoming a lie.

A necessary lie? What would have happened if I had popped up on Peter Woods's doorstep when I was in my twenties? It would have shocked and upset his wife and family and distressed my mother. It would have linked me publicly to him rather than let me make my own way in journalism. It would have been a big story at a bad moment.

So I never did it. And when, during the first Gulf War, I sat by an Egyptian army tank waiting to drive into Kuwait, and a cameraman told me about some trip he had done with Peter Woods and the fun they had had, I just kept quiet. On many other occasions too, when he was mentioned I said nothing. Like a character in a spy novel, I compartmentalised my life. And that compartment was closed and locked and buried.

And here is the point: I think it was the right thing to do. Many of the people who have been in touch with me since I wrote my piece have talked about the relief they felt when a similar secret could finally be shared. But many too have made it clear that there was a right moment for that secret to be shared, and that sometimes we have to accept that that moment might not come at all, not even on our death-beds. No man is an island. We have a responsibility one to another which transcends the "need to know" or the need to be honest and open. We live in a Wikileaks age where transparency is celebrated by some as an end in itself. This, I think, is wrong. My secret was painful and probably damaging, if I am to be brutally honest: it reduced me as a person. But the keeping of it also made me. It kept the relationship with my mother loving and fulfilling for her and me until the day she died. It protected Peter Woods and his family.

It could never have happened in America. There are two conversations that Americans are willing to have that very few Brits could or would want to match. The first is "what the pastor said in church last Sunday". Seriously, it still cracks me up that you talk about your pastors. But the second and even stranger is the conversation that begins with the words: "I was telling my analyst exactly that last Tuesday…"

From an early age, Americans are taught that to have a mental life that is not on show to someone else is a mistake. The conditioning is subtle at first but very soon becomes highly significant. "How does this make you feel?" is a question my children, growing up in America, had to get used to being asked even if their atavistic Britishness made them regard it as otiose. "Johnny hit you? And how does that make you feel?" The questions invite sarcasm, another English vice, but also invite children to explore those feelings that, frankly, they feel they should have even if they haven't. It is, in other words, an invitation to false memory syndrome. The author Gertrude Stein, returning to California and wanting to visit her childhood home, couldn't find it and declared: "There was no there there." Mentally, in America, if there is no there there, you invent a there. And you make it sound as you expect the adults will want it to sound. You embellish. You imagine. It is gloriously unhealthy and makes for some pretty messed-up children. To be frank about our children's friends at school, there were quite a few whose exploration of their inner selves was deeply damaging as well as deeply boring. I can remember one girl asking my wife Sarah: "Do you like me?" The girl was eight. It was, to use an American expression, inappropriate. Why would an eight-year-old wonder about such a thing? American culture has encouraged too much self-analysis.

Then comes adulthood and the show goes on. Several friends of ours had professional help with their innermost thoughts. Weekly sessions would explore who said what to whom when they were fourteen. Did the move to New Mexico really hurt more than it seemed at the time? Was Dad's new job never properly explained to you? This narcissism was epitomised in a book about working mothers called *Mommy Wars*, written by a friend of ours, Leslie Steiner. In it she delved, in excruciating detail, into her thoughts about her husband. The poor man has inscribed our copy thus: "Don't believe everything you read about me!" Jesus, it hardly mattered whether we did or not. The ghastly intimacy – the assumption that psychological details about your life and your unwilling partner's life are somehow better aired than not aired – is an American disaster story. It leads to an inability to cope with adversity – there is always something, someone, to blame – and it can waste huge amounts of time that would be better spent in other pursuits.

I suppose they would say that the silent approach I adopted towards my strange upbringing must have brought all sorts of hang-ups and weirdness with it, and who am I to deny it? Any sensible analysis of the English and the Americans has to acknowledge that, in every area of life, there are times when aspects of American behaviour seem superior and times when British behaviour comes out on top. In this partic-ular area I think we win: the stiff upper lip has some benefits for society generally, especially when times are tough. If the answer to the question "Who is to blame?" turns out to be "me", there is sanity to be retrieved in this uncomfortable fact. One of the big issues America faces in the coming years is whether it can avoid going to the shrink so often.

I resist the temptation to end with a grand conclu-sion about the bigger relationship between you and us. We are very different and would benefit, I think, from noting those differences more clearly. We are linked because we think we are linked but that link may be called into question and disregarded in the future. We need to be free of you and you need to be free of us. We are also – on each side of the Atlantic – facing deep fissures within our own societies. America is bold and beautiful but flawed and tawdry; Britain is steely and elegant, and after the Olympics newly self-confident, but still sometimes seems drunken and self-deluding. Having spent the best years of my professional life in America, I hold the place in the highest regard. My youngest child is a US citizen and when she becomes president I hope she has the rest of us to stay and salutes her special relationship with us. But she lives at a time when the wider special relationship has become a hindrance to clear thinking and ultimately to the continuance of the values of the English-speaking world.

We need to accept that we are different. Years ago my friend, the *Times* reporter Tim Reid, was meeting President Bush at what they call a grip-and-grin session in the White House. It was Christmas and Tim's wife Helena also came along. The amount of time you have with the great personage at these sessions is limited with even greater strictness than at a royal event. Secret service men usher you in, an announcement is made about who you are, you smile and grip and grin, a photo is taken, and you go. There is little time for small-talk.

Tim and Helena were ushered in and announced – "Mr and Mrs Tim Reid from *The Times of England!*"

President Bush, friendly and keen to please as he always was in these one-to-one events, apparently remembered that he had recently been interviewed by *The Times* of England, but here his memory understandably failed him. The interview had actually been carried out by the editor who had, by this time, hopped on a plane back to London, so when the President presented his hand to Tim and said, "Howdy, Tim, I think we met recently?", poor Tim was faced, as a quintessentially English Englishman, with a ticklish problem. How to let the President down gently? How to avoid the rudeness of a denial of their meeting but at the same time avoid going along with an untruth?

As Tim tells it, after a pause that seemed to him to be excrutiatingly long, he came up with a form of words that was both completely English and also completely barmy: "Ah, Mr President, umm, I am not sure that we actually did!"

Bush – nonplussed – turned to Helena and whispered: "You'd have thought he'd have remembered!"

How foolish we can sometimes seem to our cousins! Poor President Bush, reviled and harassed by a thousand British commentators, tries his best to be polite to a Brit he meets in the flesh and that's the thanks he gets. Truly, we are separated by so much more than our common language.

We have to let go. In 2020, we will celebrate the 400th anniversary of the *Mayflower* sailing. Already commemorative events are being planned on both sides of the Atlantic. How about an extra one? An affectionate burning of a (specially created) Grand Seal of the Special/Essential Relationship – finally, a true declaration of mutual independence.

Acknowledgements

I would like to thank the hundreds of people – public figures and private individuals – who contributed to the ideas in this book. To single out just a few: Adrian and Amelia Wooldridge, David and Genia Chavchevadze, David Frum, Sir Nigel and Lady Sheinwald, Lord and Lady McNally, Ben Preston and Janice Turner, Simon and Ulrike Wilson, Mark Damazer, Ceri Thomas, and Adi Raval, without whose Herculean efforts I would not have met and interviewed Barack Obama. I am grateful to the staff of the British Library of Political and Economic Science at the London School of Economics for their assistance with historical documents and to the Foreign Affairs Committee of the House of Commons for inviting me to speak to them about the special relationship. None of these institutions or individuals is, of course, the slightest bit responsible for anything I have got wrong. Nor is my wife, Sarah, though I should finish by thanking her for her love and support and critical reading of everything I write.

© Adi Raval

Justin Webb was named political journalist of the year for his reporting on America during Barack Obama's rise to power. He spent eight years in Washington for the BBC and one of his children is a US citizen. He is now a presenter of the *Today* programme on Radio Four.